I0824125

the Goldbergs Cookbook

the Goldbergs Cookbook

Beverly Goldberg

Written with
Jenn Fujikawa

Epilogue by
Adam F. Goldberg

UNIVERSE

THE GOLDBERGS COOKBOOK
First published in the United States of America in 2020 by
Universe Publishing, A Division of
Rizzoli International Publications, Inc.
300 Park Avenue South
New York, NY 10010
www.rizzoliusa.com

Written by Beverly Goldberg with Jenn Fujikawa
Epilogue by Adam F. Goldberg
Plated dish photography by Jenn Fujikawa

Publisher: Charles Miers
Editor: Tricia Levi
Design: Lynne Yeamans
Production Manager: Kaija Marcoe
Editorial Coordination: Robb Pearlman
Managing Editor: Lynn Scrabis

Printed in China

2020 2021 2022 2023 / 10 9 8 7 6 5 4 3

ISBN: 978-0-7893-3675-0
Library of Congress Control Number: 2019951236

Visit us online:
Facebook.com/RizzoliNewYork
Twitter: @Rizzoli_Books
Instagram.com/RizzoliBooks
Pinterest.com/RizzoliBooks
Youtube.com/user/RizzoliNY
Issuu.com/Rizzoli

Contents

Introduction

by Beverly Goldberg

Hi, everyone, and welcome to my kitchen! This book contains my most coveted recipes on the planet. Of course, a few have been exaggerated for TV because Adam enjoys nothing more than making fun of his mother. I mean, who really makes a Seven-Meat Meatloaf? In reality, mine has three meats. Which, apparently, is still two more meats than every other meatloaf.

I began cooking in 1964 when I married Murray Goldberg. I may have led him to believe I was a whiz in the kitchen, but the truth is . . . I didn't even know how to boil water. Murray loved a good home-cooked meal as his mother was fantastic in the kitchen. My first culinary venture was making a turkey for my husband and in-laws. I had no idea that it came with a bag of gizzards, which I left inside the turkey when I cooked it. You can you imagine the horror on my in-laws' faces when I cut into the turkey and discovered there was a bag stuffed with bird parts. It was also dangerously undercooked. A true f*cking disaster. By the way, I promised Adam that I'd watch my language, so that will be the one Bev bomb for this book.

I started seriously cooking for my husband and the kids in early 1970-something, because my family members were hungry people. Come five o'clock on the dot, they would all be hovering in the kitchen waiting to be fed like lost puppies. Back then, dinner was my favorite time of day. No matter what, we would drop everything to spend an hour at the table chatting and laughing—and yes,

arguing. I always loved that at the end of every meal I'd get a big thank-you and maybe even a huggy thrown in. I began creating a big collection of recipes from my mom, friends, and old cookbooks. I realized that the cookbooks from my mother's era of the 1950s all had recipes made from scratch. Just like Murray, I was obsessed with my mother's cooking. She was a stay-at-home mom who put great time and care into preparing dinner for the family. This was how I cooked in the beginning. Everything was prepared from scratch and with love.

And then 1980-something hit. There were fewer stay-at-home moms, so dinner had to be made fast and easily. During this time, I discovered a ton of new recipes on the back of food cans and boxes. While I loved making a feast from scratch, I also loved being able to whip up something quickly. Barry was a picky eater and Adam had a sensitive tummy, so I had to get creative with my dinners. This is how a lot of these crazier recipes came about. Good ol'-fashioned mom creativity and trial and error. And, of course, there was a lot of cheese. I've always been an avid cheeser. I still cheese everything to this very day. Of course, I'm watching my cholesterol nowadays, but cheese makes the meal!

I also love to bake. It's very therapeutic for me and it makes people happy. I'm known for carrying around a spare banana bread in my purse just in case I run into a friend. They started to complain to me that they were gaining weight, so I've cut back on giving out my purse loaves. Many of my mom's dessert recipes were translated by my sister, Marlene Bell. Growing up, my sister and I loved watching my mom Irene bake up a storm in our tiny kitchen. But our mother never used a measuring cup. Everything was measured by hand. So, Marlene figured out that a large pinch was a tablespoon, a palm-full was a quarter cup, and so on.

The depiction of me on *The Goldbergs* as a loving, passionate mom and cook has been a truly wonderful thank-you for the years I spent raising my kids. Cooking is how I show love and I'm thrilled I have the chance to share it with the world. This book only exists because of the many amazing fans who every day ask me for my famous shrimp parm recipe and also nagged Adam to make a cookbook. For a mama like me, it's been a true dream come true.

I wish you the best in the kitchen, from our family to yours. And to my amazing son Adam, call your mother.

—*Beverly Goldberg*

chapter 1

Bev's Parms and Casseroles

"Preheat that oven, it's parmin' time!"

—BEVERLY GOLDBERG

Bev's Meaty Baked Ziti

Season 6, Episode 20: ***This is This is Spinal Tap***

Feeding my family is my number one priority and this baked ziti might just be my number one dish. The only thing that warms my family's hearts more than one of my snuggies is a hot pan of fresh ziti. Now I coulda been a lawyer, so I used to keep this recipe under lock and key. But in this cookbook I'm giving away all my culinary secrets. And the secret to this recipe? Cheese. • *Yield: 10 servings*

16 ounces ziti pasta

2 tablespoons olive oil

1 onion, diced

2 cloves garlic, minced

1 pound ground beef

1 teaspoon garlic powder

1 teaspoon dried oregano

½ teaspoon dried basil

½ teaspoon salt

¼ teaspoon pepper

1 (26-ounce) jar or container strained tomatoes

1 (15-ounce) container ricotta cheese

2 eggs

2 cups grated Parmesan cheese

1. Preheat the oven to 350°F. Grease a 9 x 13-inch pan with nonstick spray.
2. Cook ziti according to package directions. Drain and set aside.
3. Heat olive oil in a skillet over medium-high heat. Saute the onion and garlic until soft.
4. Add the ground beef, garlic powder, oregano, basil, salt, and pepper. Cook until browned.
5. Stir in the tomatoes and simmer for 5 minutes.
6. In a bowl, stir together the ricotta, eggs, and 1 cup of the Parmesan.
7. Spread half the sauce in the bottom of the pan.
8. Top with half the cooked ziti.
9. Spread the ricotta mixture over the pasta.
10. Add the rest of the ziti on top, followed by the rest of the sauce.
11. Sprinkle the last 1 cup of Parmesan on top.
12. Bake for 30 minutes, until hot and bubbly.

Bevy's World-Class Shrimp Parm

Season 1, Episode 2: ***Daddy Daughter Day***
Season 2, Episode 3: ***The Facts of Bleeping Life***
Season 3, Episode 1: ***A Kick-Ass Risky Business Party***

If there's one meal I'm known for, it's my shrimp parm. It's a staple of The Goldberg House. My schmoos can't get enough of its fried, cheesy goodness. And over the years it's been at the center of some of my family's biggest moments. That's because it fills up their hearts as much as it fills up their tummies. • *Yield: 6 servings*

1 pound (16 to 20 count) large shrimp, cleaned and deveined

1 cup whole milk

1 cup seasoned breadcrumbs

1 cup all-purpose flour

2 teaspoons garlic powder

½ teaspoon salt

¼ teaspoon pepper

Vegetable oil for frying

1 (24-ounce) jar pasta sauce

2 cups shredded mozzarella cheese

1 cup grated Parmesan cheese

1. Preheat the oven to 350°F. Grease a 9 x 13-inch pan with nonstick spray.
2. Place the cleaned shrimp into a bowl with the milk. Set aside.
3. In a shallow dish, whisk together the breadcrumbs, flour, garlic powder, salt, and pepper.
4. Remove the shrimp from the milk and dredge them in the breading.
5. In a skillet over medium-high heat, heat 2 inches of oil, and fry the shrimp until golden brown. Transfer to paper towels to drain.
6. Pour half the sauce into the prepared pan, then layer the shrimp and half the mozzarella cheese.
7. Pour over the rest of the sauce and add the remaining mozzarella cheese.
8. Bake for 15 minutes.
9. Sprinkle Parmesan cheese on top to serve.

Cheesy Murray-Loving Sausage Casserole

Season 5, Episode 4: ***Revenge o' the Nerds***

This recipe is a Murray favorite because Murray absolutely loves sausage. Whether it's andouille or pepperoni or bratwurst, he'll eat it and he'll go back for seconds. So anytime I need him to do something for me like clean out the garage or return the paving stones to Hechingers, I just whip up my sausage casserole and Murray gets the job done. • *Yield: 8 servings*

2 pounds mild sweet Italian sausage, cut into 1-inch pieces

3 green bell peppers, cored and cut into 1-inch pieces

3 red bell peppers, cored and cut into 1-inch pieces

3 onions, cut into 1-inch pieces

1 (28-ounce) can or container tomato puree

1 teaspoon garlic powder

½ teaspoon onion powder

½ teaspoon salt

¼ teaspoon pepper

2 cups shredded mozzarella cheese

1. Preheat the oven to 350°F. Grease a 9 x 13-inch baking dish with nonstick spray.
2. In a large bowl, stir together the sausage, bell peppers, onions, and tomato puree.
3. Stir in the garlic powder, onion powder, salt, and pepper.
4. Pour into the prepared baking dish.
5. Cover the dish tightly with foil and bake for 1 hour.
6. Remove the foil and top with the cheese.
7. Set the oven to broil and place the pan under the broiler just until the cheese melts.

Cheeseburger Lasagna

Season 3, Episode 18: ***12 Tapes for a Penny***

Everyone in Jenkintown knows I make a to-die-for cheeseburger and I bake an out-of-this-world lasagna. So when I meld these two family favorites into one mind-blowing dish, it's a recipe for some very happy Goldbergs. If you want to feel special and you're craving a little thank-you from your babies, this is just the culinary combo you need. • *Yield: 8 servings*

1 (8-ounce) box lasagna noodles

1 (24-ounce) jar pasta sauce

8 leftover cheeseburger patties

1. Prepare the lasagna noodles according to package directions.
2. Preheat the oven to 350°F. Grease a 9 x 13-inch pan with nonstick spray.
3. Spread one-third of the sauce in the bottom of the pan.
4. Place one-third of the lasagna noodles on top of the sauce.
5. Add a layer of 4 cheeseburgers.
6. Top with another one-third of the lasagna noodles, then another one-third of the sauce.
7. On top of that, layer 4 more cheeseburgers, the rest of the lasagna noodles, and the rest of the sauce.
8. Bake for 15 to 20 minutes, until heated through.

Cod Parm

Season 4, Episode 1: ***Breakfast Club***

Cod Parm—it's both fishy *and* cheesy—and what's seafood without a little pizzazz? To those who say putting cheese on seafood breaks every culinary law, let me just say, I'll put cheese on anything—anything. I once cheesed a slice of watermelon. • *Yield: 8 servings*

1 cup seasoned breadcrumbs

1 cup all-purpose flour

1 teaspoon garlic powder

½ teaspoon salt

¼ teaspoon pepper

1½ pounds cod fillets

2 eggs, beaten

Vegetable oil for frying

1 (24-ounce) jar pasta sauce

2 cups shredded mozzarella cheese

1 cup grated Parmesan cheese

1. Preheat the oven to 350°F. Grease a 9 x 13-inch pan with nonstick spray.
2. In a shallow dish, whisk together the breadcrumbs, flour, garlic powder, salt, and pepper.
3. Dredge the cod in the eggs, then the dry ingredients.
4. Heat 1½ inches of oil in a skillet over medium-high heat and fry the fish until golden brown. Transfer to paper towels to drain.
5. Pour half the sauce into the prepared pan, then layer the fish and half the mozzarella cheese.
6. Top with the rest of the sauce and the remainder of the mozzarella cheese.
7. Bake for 15 minutes.
8. Sprinkle Parmesan cheese on top to serve.

"I love Barry, but he ruins everything."

—BEVERLY GOLDBERG

Bev's Bevolutionary Crab Parm

Season 5, Episode 4: ***Revenge o' the Nerds***

When my kids started heading off to college, I knew it was time for a Bevolution. I was ready to reinvent myself and that meant reinventing some of my favorite recipes. That's when I discovered crab was the perfect ocean meat for parming. So when I mastered this recipe, my kids couldn't stay away. • *Yield: 8 servings*

1½ pounds crab meat

¼ cup seasoned breadcrumbs

⅔ cup mayonnaise

1 teaspoon garlic powder

½ teaspoon salt, plus more as needed

¼ teaspoon pepper, plus more as needed

1 cup all-purpose flour

Vegetable oil for frying

1 (24-ounce) jar pasta sauce

2 cups shredded mozzarella cheese

1 cup grated Parmesan cheese

1. Preheat the oven to 350°F. Grease a 9 x 13-inch pan with nonstick spray.
2. In a large bowl, mix together the crab meat, breadcrumbs, mayonnaise, garlic powder, salt, and pepper.
3. Form into hamburger-sized patties.
4. In a shallow dish, season the flour with salt and pepper.
5. Dredge the crab cake patties in the flour mixture to coat, shaking off the excess.
6. Heat 2 inches of oil in a skillet over medium-high heat and fry the crab cakes until golden brown. Let drain.
7. Pour half the sauce into the prepared pan, then layer the crab cakes and half the mozzarella cheese.
8. Top with the rest of the sauce and the remainder of the mozzarella cheese.
9. Bake for 15 minutes.
10. Sprinkle Parmesan cheese on top to serve.

Parming Like a Pro

Cod Parm, Crab Parm, Eggplant Parm, it's always a Parm roulette when it comes to dinnertime. In the end, there's no denying that Shrimp Parm is the ultimate Parm. It's the best dish for celebrating, for grieving, for calming anger—think of it as the mood ring of foods.

To cheese up the shrimp just right you need the correct temperature of oil: 360°F is ideal; if you don't have a thermometer, simply sprinkle a few breadcrumbs into the hot oil. If they pop and sizzle in their own little jazzercisey way, you're good to go.

Lay on the sauce and go heavy on the cheese; in other words, don't hold back. Think of a perfect parm like matchmaking. Shrimp and cheese may seem like an odd match, but in the end the two form a perfect union full of delicious love.

Doctor-Approved Eggplant Parm

SEASON 4, EPISODE 12: ***Snow Day***

If you're health conscious, you might think there's nothing in *The Goldbergs Cookbook* for you. But feast your eyes on my Doctor-Approved Eggplant Parm. There's no meat, so you keep your calories down. Though that leaves extra room for cheese, so your doctor might not approve after all. But who needs him anyway? My schmoopaloos are gonna be doctors and I know they approve. • *Yield: 8 servings*

4 purple eggplants, peeled and sliced thin

½ teaspoon salt, plus more for salting eggplant slices

1 cup seasoned breadcrumbs

1 cup all-purpose flour

1 teaspoon garlic powder

¼ teaspoon pepper

4 eggs, lightly beaten

Vegetable oil for frying

2 (24-ounce) jars pasta sauce

2 cups shredded mozzarella cheese

2 cups grated Parmesan cheese

1. Sprinkle the eggplant slices with salt and then layer them between paper towels.
2. In a shallow bowl, whisk the breadcrumbs, flour, garlic powder, salt, and pepper. Set aside.
3. Pat the eggplant slices dry, dip them into the egg, then dredge in the breadcrumb mixture.
4. Heat 1 inch of oil in a skillet over medium-high heat and fry the eggplant until golden brown. Transfer to paper towels to drain.
5. Preheat the oven to 350°F. Grease a 9 x 13-inch pan with nonstick spray.
6. Layer the eggplant in the prepared pan and bake for 10 minutes.
7. Remove from the oven and pour over the pasta sauce, then sprinkle on the mozzarella cheese.
8. Place back in the oven and cook for 30 minutes.
9. Sprinkle Parmesan cheese on top to serve.

Creamy Supreme Tater Tot Casserole

Some say mankind's greatest achievement was putting a man on the moon, but I say it was the invention of the tater tot. And in this recipe, I've taken the tot and combined it with the cream of the gods. I'm talking, of course, about cream of mushroom soup. It's tots and mushrooms casseroled into one supremely satisfying dish. • *Yield: 8 servings*

Butter, for greasing

1 pound ground beef

½ cup diced onion

1 tablespoon Worcestershire sauce

½ teaspoon garlic powder

½ teaspoon onion powder

½ teaspoon salt

¼ teaspoon pepper

1 (14.5-ounce) can green beans, drained

1 (10.5-ounce) can cream of mushroom soup

1½ cups shredded cheddar cheese

1 (32-ounce) package frozen tater tots

Parsley for decoration

Sour cream for serving

1. Preheat the oven to 375°F. Grease a 9 x 13-inch baking pan with butter.
2. In a skillet over medium-high heat, brown the ground beef and onion.
3. Stir in the Worcestershire sauce, garlic powder, onion powder, salt, and pepper and cook for 2 to 3 minutes. Remove the fat from the skillet.
4. Stir in the green beans and cream of mushroom soup, then pour everything into the prepared pan.
5. Sprinkle with the cheese, then arrange the tater tots on top of the casserole.
6. Bake for 40 minutes.
7. Sprinkle parsley for decoration and serve with dollops of sour cream.

Tuna Picasso

SEASON 4, EPISODE 23: ***Jedi Master Adam Skywalker***

This is my masterpiece. If the *Mona Lisa* were a casserole she'd be this one, and she'd be smiling about it. I don't think I'm bragging when I say I'm the Da'Vinci of Da'casseroles. The pan is my canvas, the ingredients my paints, and the finished product should be put in a museum. But then take it out of the museum, heat it up in the microwave, and serve! • *Yield: 8 servings*

2 (10.5-ounce) cans cream of mushroom soup

1 (12-ounce) can tuna, drained and flaked

3 cups crushed potato chips

1 cup cooked green peas

1 cup whole milk

1. Preheat the oven to 350°F. Grease a 9 x 13-inch pan with nonstick spray.
2. In a bowl, mix together the soup, tuna, 2 cups of the crushed potato chips, peas, and milk.
3. Pour into the prepared pan.
4. Sprinkle the remaining 1 cup crushed potato chips on top.
5. Bake for 25 minutes, until browned.

"I have failed as a mother."

chapter 2

Mostly Meaty Family Faves

"Do you know how many meals I have cooked for you people? 53,000!"

—BEVERLY GOLDBERG

Hearty Seven-Meat Meatloaf

Season 3, Episode 7: *Lucky*

When I was just a girl and made my first meatloaf, I had questions. And the biggest question was "why stop at one meat when you can have seven?" Yes, some might say it's out of control. It goes against nature. But I say just give it a taste and then the only question you'll have is "can I have seconds?" • *Yield: 10 servings*

Vegetable oil for greasing

½ pound ground beef

½ pound ground veal

4 slices bacon, cooked and chopped

1 cup seasoned breadcrumbs

2 eggs

1 tablespoon Worcestershire sauce

Salt and pepper

1 pound ground pork

½ pound ground turkey

¼ teaspoon celery seed

½ pound ground chicken

¼ teaspoon garlic powder

6 ounces Italian sausage, chopped

¾ cup ketchup

2 tablespoons brown sugar

1. Preheat the oven to 375°F. Lightly grease an 8 x 8-inch baking pan with oil.
2. In a bowl, combine the ground beef, ground veal, cooked bacon, ½ cup of the breadcrumbs, one of the eggs, Worcestershire sauce, salt, and pepper. Set aside.
3. In a second bowl, combine the ground pork, the remaining ½ cup breadcrumbs, and the remaining egg.
4. In a third bowl, combine the ground turkey and celery seed, then season with salt and pepper.
5. In a fourth and final bowl, combine the ground chicken with the garlic powder, then season with salt and pepper.
6. Press half the ground beef and veal mixture into the bottom of the prepared pan.
7. Layer half of the pork mixture on top.
8. Evenly press the ground turkey mixture over the pork.

9. Sprinkle the Italian sausage over the turkey layer.
10. Press the ground chicken mixture on top and season with salt and pepper.
11. Layer the remaining half of the pork mixture on top, then end with the rest of the ground beef mixture.
12. Cook for 1 hour and 45 minutes, or until an instant-read thermometer registers 165°F.
13. Spread the ketchup over the top and sprinkle on the brown sugar.
14. Bake for another 10 to 15 minutes.
15. Let rest for 5 to 10 minutes, then slice to serve.

Big Tasty Pork for My Big Tasty Babies

SEASON 2, EPISODE 8: ***I Rode a Hoverboard***

I know a lot of people think it's just easier to eat out than cook, but I hate it. Why pay when you have the best food right in your kitchen? But if you *do* go out, I like to take it as an opportunity to see what else is out there and then steal the recipe and pass it off as my own. And that's just what I did when I tried Dave Kim's mom's pork dish! • *Yield: 6 servings*

For the fried pork chops:

Vegetable oil for frying

1 egg

1 teaspoon soy sauce

½ cup rice flour

1 teaspoon Chinese five-spice powder

½ teaspoon salt

¼ teaspoon white pepper

6 thin boneless pork chops

Make the fried pork chops:

1. Heat the oil in a skillet over medium-high heat.
2. In a shallow dish, beat the egg with the soy sauce. Set aside.
3. In a separate shallow dish, whisk the rice flour, Chinese five spice, salt, and pepper.
4. Dip the pork chops in the egg mixture, then in the flour mixture, shaking off the excess.
5. Fry until golden brown and cooked through. Set aside.

For the stir-fried pork:

2 tablespoons soy sauce

1 tablespoon rice vinegar

1 clove garlic, minced

¼-inch-slice fresh ginger

1 tablespoon vegetable oil

½ pound ground pork

1 cup snow peas

1 tablespoon cornstarch

Make the stir-fried pork:

1. In a bowl, stir together the soy sauce, rice vinegar, garlic, and ginger. Set aside.
2. Heat the oil in a skillet over medium-high heat. Add the pork and brown it.
3. Add the snow peas and the soy sauce mixture. Simmer for 5 minutes.
4. In a small bowl, stir together 2 tablespoons water and the cornstarch. Pour into the pan, bring to a boil, and let boil until the sauce is thickened. Discard the ginger.
5. Spoon the ground pork mixture over the fried pork chops to serve.

Cheeseburger Meatloaf

Season 2, Episode 8: ***I Rode a Hoverboard***

Once I discovered I could combine cheeseburger and lasagna, I started to wonder what other dishes I could mash together in the name of dinner science. That's when I invented my cheeseburger lasagna. It's got all that cheese-y burger-y deliciousness with fewer noodles and more meat. Adam devoured so much of it, he was begging for belly rubs and I was more than happy to serve them up. •

Yield: 8 servings

For the meatloaf:

Vegetable oil for greasing

2½ pounds ground beef

½ cup diced onion

½ cup plain breadcrumbs

¼ cup grated Parmesan cheese

2 eggs, lightly beaten

1½ tablespoons Worcestershire sauce

1 teaspoon garlic powder

½ teaspoon onion powder

½ teaspoon salt

¼ teaspoon pepper

For finishing:

10 slices American cheese

⅓ cup ketchup

5 frozen onion rings, baked

Make the meatloaf:

1. Preheat the oven to 375°F. Lightly grease a loaf pan with oil.
2. In a bowl combine the beef, onion, breadcrumbs, Parmesan cheese, eggs, Worcestershire sauce, garlic powder, onion powder, salt, and pepper.
3. Press the beef mixture into the loaf pan.
4. Bake for 70 to 80 minutes, or until the internal temperature reaches 160°F.
5. Let rest for 5 minutes, then cut the meatloaf into thirds lengthwise.

Finish the meatloaf:

1. On a serving platter, place 5 slices of cheese on top of the bottom layer of meatloaf, stack the second layer of meat, add 5 more slices cheese, then top with the last layer of meat.
2. Spread the ketchup on top and add the onion rings to serve.

Heavyweight Champion Lasagna

SEASON 4, EPISODE 8: ***The Greatest Musical Ever Written***

Now cooking isn't a competition, but if it were, my lasagna could take yours any day. Not only does it have a winning taste, but it's also a heavyweight champ clocking in at a solid 15 to 20 pounds of cheesy, meaty, noodle-y deliciousness. And when you make this for your family, get ready, because they'll be coming back for round two. • *Yield: 15 servings*

3 tablespoons vegetable oil

1 pound ground beef

1 pound ground veal

1 pound ground pork

1 (16-ounce) box lasagna noodles

2 (15-ounce) containers ricotta cheese

6 eggs

2 tablespoons garlic powder

2 teaspoons onion powder

2 teaspoons dried oregano

1 teaspoon salt

½ teaspoon pepper

3 (24-ounce) jars pasta sauce

8 cups shredded mozzarella cheese

2 cups grated Parmesan cheese

1. Heat the oil in a large skillet over medium-high heat. Add the beef, veal, and pork and brown them. Set aside.
2. Prepare the lasagna noodles according to package directions.
3. Preheat the oven to 375°F.
4. In a large bowl, mix together the ricotta cheese, eggs, garlic powder, onion powder, oregano, salt, and pepper.
5. Pour a jar of pasta sauce into the bottom of a 6-quart 13 x 16-inch baking pan.
6. Layer the lasagna noodles, the ricotta mixture, meat, then mozzarella. Repeat until you're out of ingredients, ending with the sauce.
7. Cover with aluminum foil and bake for 30 minutes.
8. Remove the foil, top with the Parmesan cheese, and bake for another 15 minutes.

Mama's Mouthwatering Meatloaf Burgers

Season 6, Episode 2: ***You Got Zuko'd***

Now I've already introduced you to my cheeseburger meatloaf, but what about my meatloaf burgers? The difference here is you're taking all the delicious heartwarming taste of a meatloaf dinner and you're putting it in the on-the-go form of a burger—except when you try these meatloaf burgers, you won't want to go anywhere. • *Yield: 6 servings*

1 pound ground beef

½ pound ground pork

½ pound ground veal

½ cup plain breadcrumbs

½ cup diced onion

1 egg

¼ cup whole milk

1 tablespoon ketchup

2 teaspoons garlic powder

Salt and pepper

Hamburger buns, toasted

Lettuce

Tomato

1. Preheat the oven to 375°F.
2. In a large bowl, mix together the ground beef, pork, veal, and the breadcrumbs, onion, egg, milk, ketchup, garlic powder, salt, and pepper.
3. Form 6 patties and place them on a baking sheet.
4. Bake for 25 minutes.
5. Serve on the toasted buns with lettuce and tomato.

"No one tells my baby he can't cobra strike!"

Monte Cristo Sandwich

Season 1, Episode 1: ***Circle of Driving***

Murray adores Monte Cristo sandwiches. They are beyond high in cholesterol and fat but it's 1980-something and this is how we eat. Now for most people this kind of sandwich is for special occasions only, but in The Goldberg House every day is a special occasion. • *Yield: 1 serving*

8 ounces pastrami

2 slices rye bread

¼ cup sauerkraut

2 slices Swiss cheese

4 tablespoons (½ stick) unsalted butter

2 eggs, beaten

1. Place the pastrami on a slice of rye bread. Top with the sauerkraut, then cheese, then the other slice of bread.
2. Melt the butter in a skillet over medium-high heat.
3. Dip the sandwich into the beaten eggs, then place it in the pan.
4. Cook until golden brown, then flip over and brown the other side.
5. Serve immediately.

Shopping Like a Pro

When it comes to meals, planning isn't always in the cards. Sometimes a family's busy schedule becomes the determining factor. One minute you could be spending hours shuttling the kids to hockey practice; the next heading to band camp or your kid's amateur performance of *Starlight Express*. With an itinerary like that, it's always best to have everything you need so that you can whip up any culinary masterpiece on a whim. I even like to keep a small portable deli counter in the car glove compartment, in case Barry's blood sugar gets low.

- **To be able to cook anything on demand means you'll need a fully stocked pantry.** That's why certain essentials are a must when hitting up the grocery store. No cheap, bargain meat will do when it comes to feeding the loves of your lives. Ask for the highest-quality cuts, and always check to see if they've got special meats in the back. Hidden meat is the best meat.

- **As far as dairy, Parmesan should be at the top of every shopping list.** You never know when you'll want to parm. Heavy dairy like buttermilk is a miracle ingredient: not only can it coat your tum-tum before an afternoon of sporting activities, but it can also serve as a base for incredibly rich, coma-inducing meals. And whatever you don't use can easily be whipped into a nice butterscotch pudding.

- **Ecto Cooler will probably be around forever, but it's best to stock up so that you'll always have a juice box on hand.** Need a boost? No problem. Jolt Cola is good to keep in the fridge for those late-night jam sessions and unexpected high-energy karate performances. Snapple Tru Root Beer, now that's a good soda. Anytime my Adam has a big test, I don't let him leave the house without a root beer from the good people at Snapple. They just really know how to make soda and no other type of drink. Oh, and of course Apple Slice. As if my kids didn't already love Slice enough, now there's an apple flavor, which makes me feel like it's healthy even though the can specifically says, "Does not contain any actual fruit products."

- **In the end, you can meal plan as much as you want, but the best advice is to buy ingredients that let you cook from the heart.** When you're doing your grocery shopping, keep in mind that dinner is not just dinner—dinner makes you feel needed—and cooking for family means everything.

Scrumptious Short Rib Potpie (No Peas, No Carrots)

SEASON 5, EPISODE 18: *MTV Spring Break*

Everyone loves a potpie, but not everyone loves when they're stuffed full of peas and carrots, including my Murray. Murray refuses to eat a single veggie, so that's why I came up with my Short Rib Potpie. When you lose the peas and carrots you gain a whole bunch of room for more savory short rib. • *Yield: 6 servings*

2 pounds boneless beef short ribs

1½ tablespoons salt

1 teaspoon pepper

¼ cup all-purpose flour

2 tablespoons olive oil

1 tablespoon unsalted butter

½ onion, sliced

2 cloves garlic, minced

1 (10-ounce) can beef broth

1 teaspoon Worcestershire sauce

Prepared pie dough, store-bought

1 egg plus 1 teaspoon water for egg wash

Salt for sprinkling

1. Season the short ribs with salt and pepper. Dredge in the flour.
2. In a Dutch oven over medium-high heat, add the olive oil and the butter and brown the short ribs. Remove and set aside.
3. Add the onion and garlic to the Dutch oven and cook until soft, scraping the bits off the bottom of the pot.
4. Place the ribs back in the pot and pour in the beef broth and Worcestershire sauce.
5. Simmer on low for 2 hours.
6. Preheat the oven to 375°F.
7. Transfer the meat and onions to a pie plate.
8. Roll out the pie dough and place the dough over the filling, crimping the edges. Cut slits to vent.
9. Brush with egg wash, then sprinkle with salt.
10. Bake for 30 minutes, until golden brown.

The Bevernator's Stir-Fry Spectacular

SEASON 1, EPISODE 7: ***Call Me When You Get There***

Ah stir-fry. This may be an exotic dish from across the globe, but I put my Bevernator spin on it and turn it into a Goldberg must. All the vegetables make it healthy but the key to this crowd-pleaser is the oil. Though be careful to avoid fires because this recipe gets steamy fast. • *Yield: 2 servings*

3 tablespoons olive oil

2 bell peppers, cored and cut into a large dice

1 onion, cut into a large dice

1 cup broccoli florets

8 ounces sliced mushrooms

1 carrot, shredded

1 medium eggplant, peeled and cubed

1 yellow squash, cubed

2 teaspoons garlic powder

1 cup shrimp, chicken, or beef, cubed

½ cup sliced almonds

1 cup cooked rice

1 tablespoon bottled Asian dressing, or more to your preference

1. In a large skillet over medium-high heat, saute the vegetables in one tablespoon of the olive oil. Sprinkle with 1 teaspoon of the garlic powder, and cook the vegetables until softened, about 5 minutes. Remove and set aside.
2. In the same pan, add the second tablespoon of olive oil and the shrimp. Sprinkle with the other teaspoon of garlic powder and saute the shrimp until cooked through. Remove and set aside.
3. Toast the almonds in the pan for 1 to 2 minutes. Remove and set aside as well.
4. Add the final tablespoon of olive oil and the cooked rice. Cook until just crisp.
5. Return the vegetables, shrimp, and nuts to the pan. Toss lightly with the rice and dressing.

Classic Schmoopie Schnitzel

Again with the fried? Yes! Schnitzel is a classic: savory meat, coated, fried, and served up crispy and delicious. Serve this to your schmoopies as the ultimate sign of a mama's delicious love. • *Yield: 8 servings*

8 boneless skinless chicken breasts, pounded thin

½ cup all-purpose flour

2 eggs

2 tablespoons soy sauce

1 cup plain breadcrumbs

¼ cup sesame seeds

1 teaspoon paprika

½ teaspoon garlic salt

½ teaspoon salt

Vegetable oil for frying

Apricot preserves, warmed

1. Preheat the oven to 350°F. Grease a 9 x 13-inch baking sheet with nonstick spray.
2. Create a breading station with three dishes, placing flour in the first dish.
3. In the second dish whisk together the eggs, soy sauce, and 2 tablespoons water.
4. In the last dish stir together the breadcrumbs, sesame seeds, paprika, garlic salt, and salt.
5. Coat a large skillet with oil and set over medium-high heat.
6. Dredge the chicken in the flour, shaking off the excess. Then dip the breasts into the egg mixture, and finally coat them in the breadcrumbs. Cook the chicken in the skillet until just browned. Let drain on a wire rack, then transfer to the prepared baking sheet.
7. Bake for 45 minutes. Serve with the warmed apricot preserves.

Tender-Loving Brisket

SEASON 5, EPISODE 22: *Let's Val Kilmer This Car*

I present to you the most tender brisket ever brisketed. While this does take two days, I promise you it's worth it. And the secret to the perfect brisket? Skinny slices. They make all the difference. I even like to bring my already cooked brisket to the deli counter and have them slice it for me. They see me coming and say, "Uh oh. Here comes Mrs. Goldberg. We better rev up the industrial slicer for her extra-thin slices." • *Yield: 10 servings*

2 onions, sliced

2 (8-ounce) containers sliced mushrooms

2 tablespoons vegetable oil

3 to 4 pounds beef brisket

2 envelopes onion soup mix

5 carrots, peeled and sliced

3 potatoes, peeled and cubed

1. In a skillet over medium-high heat, saute the onions and mushrooms in the oil for 10 to 12 minutes. Set aside.
2. Preheat the oven to 350°F.
3. Place the brisket in a Dutch oven. Add the onion soup mix and the sauteed onions and mushrooms. Pour in enough water to just cover the brisket (approximately 2 cups), then cover with foil. Place in the oven.
4. After 1 hour, lift the foil and add another 1 cup water and add the carrots and potatoes. Close the foil around the Dutch oven.
5. Continue to cook for 3 hours, lifting the foil and adding a cup of water every hour.

6. Pull the brisket out of the oven and let cool slightly, then let it cool completely in the refrigerator overnight.
7. Remove the carrots and potatoes and set aside.
8. Remove the brisket and slice thin. Set aside.
9. Bring the remaining contents of the Dutch oven to a boil to make gravy.
10. Place the sliced brisket, potatoes, and carrots back into the gravy and reduce the heat to a simmer.
11. Once the meat and vegetables are heated through, the brisket is ready to serve.

chapter 3

From Bev with Love

"Sorry I annoyed you with my unconditional love and support of everything you do."

—BEVERLY GOLDBERG

Barry's Own Butter Cookies

SEASON 4, EPISODE 8: ***The Greatest Musical Ever Written***

My Barry not only loves my cooking, but he's been known to put on his chef's hat from time to time as well. So he was the brains behind these delectable butter cookies. Though I may have perfected the recipe, he gave me his Barry blessing. • *Yield: 24 cookies*

2 cups all-purpose flour

1 teaspoon baking powder

¼ teaspoon salt

¾ cup (1½ sticks) unsalted butter, softened

1 cup sugar plus ½ cup sugar for dipping

1 egg

1½ teaspoons vanilla extract

½ cup milk, for dipping

1. Preheat the oven to 375°F. Line baking sheets with parchment paper.
2. In a bowl whisk together the flour, baking powder, and salt. Set aside.
3. In the bowl of a stand mixer with a beater attachment, cream the butter and 1 cup of the sugar.
4. Add in the egg and vanilla and mix until combined.
5. Beat in the flour mixture until well blended.
6. Shape the dough into 1-inch balls. Dip each ball halfway into the milk, then into the remaining ½ cup sugar. Place on the prepared baking sheets.
7. Bake for 10 to 12 minutes, until lightly browned. Let cool on a wire rack.

BORP

Beverly's Ol' Raisins and Peanuts

Season 6, Episode 23: ***Breakin'***

Before Erica went back to college, she went a little cuckoo and decided it was a good idea to spend the entire summer following the Grateful Dead around in a van. Well, if she was going to make a questionable decision, at least she shouldn't have to eat questionable food. That's where my salty-sweet BORP comes in. This snack is a road trip to yummy-town. • *Yield: 16 servings*

2 cups dry roasted peanuts
2 cups pretzels
2 cups M&Ms
1 cup Skittles
1 cup cashews
1 cup raisins
½ cup caramel chips

1. In a large bowl, stir all the ingredients together.
2. Spoon into individual containers to serve.

"Schmoopaloos! Exciting news!"

Bev's Bananas Banana Bread

Season 4, Episode 18: ***Baré***

My schmoopie-poos love this bread, which I make at least once a week. Anything to make them happy. • *Yield: 10 servings*

1½ cups all-purpose flour

1 teaspoon baking soda

½ cup (1 stick) unsalted butter, softened

1¼ cups sugar

4 ripe bananas, mashed

2 eggs

1 teaspoon vanilla extract

¼ cup sour cream

½ cup walnuts, chopped

¼ cup dark chocolate chips

1. Preheat the oven to 350°F. Grease a 5 x 9-inch loaf pan with nonstick spray.
2. In a small bowl, mix together the flour and baking soda.
3. In a large bowl, mix together the butter, sugar, bananas, eggs, and vanilla.
4. Alternate adding the sour cream with the flour and baking soda mixture.
5. Fold in the walnuts and chocolate chips.
6. Pour into the prepared pan.
7. Bake for 1½ hours, until a toothpick inserted in the center comes out clean.
8. Let cool, then slice to serve.

Mac and Cheese Meatballs

Season 2, Episode 8: ***I Rode a Hoverboard***

Mac and Cheese Meatballs can turn anyone into a cheese lover. Fabulous hunks of meat encasing gooey, cheesy macaroni. It's an entrée *and* a side, combined into one super-satisfying super-dish! There's nothing like it and that's exactly why my family likes it. • *Yield: 12 meatballs*

1 (7.25-ounce) box Macaroni & Cheese

1 pound ground beef

½ pound ground pork

½ pound ground veal

2 teaspoons garlic powder

½ teaspoon salt

¼ teaspoon pepper

2 tablespoons olive oil

1 (24-ounce) jar pasta sauce

1. Make the macaroni and cheese according to the package directions. Set aside 1½ cups for the meatballs and save the rest for snacks.
2. In a large bowl, mix together the ground beef, pork, and veal, and the garlic powder, salt, and pepper.
3. Use approximately 2½ tablespoons of meat to form a meatball around 1 heaping tablespoon of mac and cheese, sealing tightly. Repeat with the remaining meatball mixture and mac and cheese to form 12 meatballs.
4. Heat the oil in a large skillet over medium-high heat. Add the meatballs and brown them in the oil.
5. Pour over the pasta sauce, then cover and simmer for 10 to 12 minutes, until the meatballs are cooked through.

Couponing Like a Pro

Couponing is more than a hobby, it's a sport. No, it's a way of life. Finding that deal where you can double your coupon and double your savings is a joy that comes second to giving birth to your beloved children.

- **Any master of all bargain hunters knows that organization is the key to grabbing the deals.**
  Clipping takes hours and you don't want those savings flying away. A proper coupon pouch is a good first step, and once you go pro you can move on to a savings satchel. And maybe one day, when you're ready, you can don a frugal fanny pack.

- **The unequivocal rule of couponing: stay focused.**
  Don't get sidelined by fancy twofers or buy five, get ten free items. The point of couponing is to find savings on things you actually want and need. In other words, just because you have a coupon for canned bananas, doesn't mean you should buy them.

Eggy in the Heart

Season 5, Episode 2: ***Hogan Is My Grandfather***
Season 6, Episode 13: ***I Coulda Been a Lawyer***

The best way to kick off my boofaloos' morning is a hearty breakfast topped off with a heaping pile of a mama's love. And I've found that the best breakfast is a heart-shaped Eggy in the Hole. It's scrumptious and it fills the eggy-shaped hole my babies leave in my heart. • *Yield: 1 serving*

You'll need:

Heart-shaped cookie cutter

1 slice bread

1 tablespoon unsalted butter

1 egg

1 tablespoon grated Parmesan cheese

Salt and pepper

1. Use the cutter to cut a hole from the center of the bread.
2. Melt the butter in a skillet over medium-high heat and add the bread along with the cut-out heart piece.
3. Crack the egg into the hole in the bread. Cook for 2 minutes or until the white is set.
4. Sprinkle with the Parmesan cheese, salt, and pepper.
5. Serve with the toasted bread heart on the side.

"You just keep being delicious."

Bran Muffins to Help You Make

Season 6, Episode 13: ***I Coulda Been a Lawyer***

Part of a mother's job is not only making sure good things go into a growing boy's body, but also that only good things come out. Well, from time to time my Adam's bottom gets stopped up and when that happens I just whip up a batch of my delicious bran muffins. That always does the trick and tastes delightful in the process. • *Yield: 12 servings*

2 cups all-bran cereal

½ cup vanilla yogurt

2 ripe bananas, mashed

1 cup all-purpose flour

½ cup packed brown sugar

1 tablespoon baking powder

½ teaspoon ground cinnamon

Pinch of salt

¼ cup vegetable oil

1 egg

1. In a medium bowl, stir together the bran cereal, yogurt, and bananas. Set aside.
2. Preheat the oven to 375°F. Place liners in a 12-cup muffin tin.
3. In a separate large bowl whisk together the flour, brown sugar, baking powder, cinnamon, and salt.
4. Make a well in the center of the dry ingredients and stir in the bran mixture, oil, and egg until just combined.
5. Spoon the batter into the prepared muffin tin and bake for 15 to 18 minutes, until a toothpick inserted in the center of a muffin comes out clean.
6. Let cool on a wire rack.

Frenta French Toast Soufflé

SEASON 6, EPISODE 17: ***Our Perfect Strangers***

The perfect brunch requires two ingredients: my to-die-for French toast and a group of best friends to enjoy it. I treat my frentas—friend yentas—to this succulent soufflé-style French toast, and it's such a hit we almost forget to catch up on all the neighborhood gossip. Almost. • *Yield: 8 servings*

10 cups (approximately 16 slices) cubed, crustless white bread

1 (8-ounce) package cream cheese

8 eggs

1½ cups low-fat milk

⅔ cup half-and-half

½ cup maple syrup plus more for serving

½ teaspoon vanilla extract

2 tablespoons powdered sugar

1. Grease a 9 x 13-inch baking dish with nonstick spray.
2. Place the bread cubes in the prepared dish.
3. In a bowl, use a hand mixer to beat the cream cheese until smooth.
4. Add the eggs one at a time, mixing well after each addition.
5. Stir in the milk, half-and-half, the maple syrup, and vanilla until smooth.
6. Pour the cream cheese mixture over the bread cubes, cover, and refrigerate overnight.
7. Remove the baking dish from the refrigerator and let sit at room temperature for 30 minutes.
8. Preheat the oven to 375°F, then bake for 50 minutes.
9. Sprinkle with powdered sugar and serve with maple syrup.

10 Rules for Eating Out

Dinner with the Goldbergs is all about rules—very specific, non-negotiable rules—all of which should be followed to a T for a perfect meal. Whether you're going to Beefsteak Charlies for a huge slab of meat or celebrating Clam-uary at Red Lobster, it's imperative that you make the most of the night by ordering precisely, strong-arming your waiter, not filling up on appetizers, sending back food, and, most important, holding steadfast to your principles.

RULE 1: A Good Table

Don't settle when it comes to seating. Anything next to the kitchen is a garbage table. Under the air conditioner? That's a surefire way to get pneumonia. Check for echoes: there's nothing like not being able to hear yourself think when you are trying to decide what to eat. Booths are a definite no, especially when your husband has a bad back. He has to sit in a chair like a human being. Check the table for wobbles—rattling silverware is a distraction.

RULE 2: Hold the Bread

Bread should be eaten sparingly. I only let Murray have it when he gets shaky hungry and I can tell his blood sugar is plummeting. Otherwise, the bread basket is off-limits. No need to fill your tummy up with tasty rolls when there's a big meal ahead. That's what large handbags are for, so load those toasty treats into your foil-lined food purse!

RULE 3: Free Refills

Always go for the free refill. Bottomless soda means all you can drink, all night long. But the trick is only order one soda for the whole family—you're not made of money. So one communal soda for the table is how you beat the system.

RULE 4: Ordering the Murray Way

Menu rules are simple—it's all about cost saving. No prime cuts, no fancy sides, no out-of-season vegetables, no market price, no salad bar, no items in French, no dry-aged anything. But, most important, no appetizers of any kind because that's how they screw you. And that definitely includes soups. I mean, you're gonna eat a little water meal before a big meal? How many meals do you need?

RULE 5: Ask for What You Want

Think of the menu as just a vague suggestion. Just because it's written in ink, doesn't mean substitutions aren't possible. When in doubt, shrimp it out. If the meal comes with a vegetable medley, see if instead of asparagus, they'll sub in six pieces of shrimp. Adjusting to your palate is also a must. Ask for the hanger steak, Pittsburgh-style, but instead of the béarnaise sauce, get the crab cakes. It doesn't hurt to ask.

RULE 6: Free Cake

Birthdays mean free cake and that means every time the Goldbergs eat out, it's someone's birthday. Even if it's not your birthday, the odds are you were born within the last 364 days and that's not nothing. Free cake is all about celebrating the day your mama pushed you out of her swimsuit area.

RULE 7: The Food You Deserve

Watch every other table like a hawk so you'll know when your food will arrive. If you happen to see what vaguely looks like your order heading to another table, run the interception and grab that food!

RULE 8: Quantity Over Quality

Let's face it, big portions are why you go out to eat in the first place. Even if you make a bad judgment and order fish at a steakhouse, you can't deny that a large portion makes it worth it. This is why you stayed away from the bread basket in the first place.

RULE 9: Send It Back

Regardless of the fact that you've taken a bite (or two, or three), there's no shame in sending back for new meat. Much like the menu, the food itself is a suggestion. Don't forget to ask for a doggie bag for the food you're sending back. It may not be what you like, but there's no sense letting it go to waste.

RULE 10: Check the Bill Like an Accountant

Better yet, check the bill like a detective, always on the lookout for any fast ones the restaurant might be pulling on you. Is that an extra Coke I see? Did they charge for a side salad at an entrée price? What about that salmon Erica returned because she said it tasted "too fishy"?

French Onion Schwartz

SEASON 5, EPISODE 12: ***Dinner with the Goldbergs***

My daughter's boyfriend, Geoff, used to say he loved his mother Linda's French onion soup. Then he tried mine. Let's just say be careful who you cook this for because it's bound to steal hearts and children. • *Yield: 4 servings*

½ cup (1 stick) unsalted butter

8 large onions, sliced

1 envelope onion soup mix

1 (14.5-ounce) can beef broth

4 slices French bread, toasted

4 thick slices Provolone cheese

1. Melt the butter in a skillet over medium heat. Saute the onions in the butter until translucent. Set aside.
2. In a large pot, bring 3½ cups water to a boil, then reduce the heat to low and stir in the onion soup mix, sauteed onions, and beef broth. Simmer for 1 hour.
3. Preheat the oven broiler.
4. Place 4 ovenproof soup bowls on a baking sheet and divide the soup among them.
5. Top each with a slice of bread, then a slice of cheese.
6. Put the baking sheet in the oven and broil until the cheese is just browned.

"I would like the hanger steak, Pittsburgh-style, but instead of the béarnaise sauce, I would like crab cakes."

—BEVERLY GOLDBERG

Bevernator Power Chili

SEASON 3, EPISODE 21: *Rush*

Some say a heavy meal will slow you down—but Mom knows best. A big bowl of meat and beans washed down with some bone-strengthening buttermilk will give you all the energy you need before a big game. Feel the beefy power! • *Yield: 10 servings*

4 slices bacon, diced

2 pounds ground beef

2 onions, diced

4 cloves garlic, minced

1 (28-ounce) can stewed tomatoes

2 (8-ounce) cans tomato sauce

1 (14.5-ounce) can kidney beans

5 tablespoons chili powder

2 teaspoons garlic salt

2 teaspoons ground oregano

2 teaspoons ground cumin

½ teaspoon pepper

1. In a skillet over medium-high heat, cook the bacon until crispy. Transfer to paper towels to drain and set aside.
2. Pour out the excess grease, then brown the beef, onions, and garlic.
3. Stir in the stewed tomatoes, tomato sauce, kidney beans, chili powder, garlic salt, oregano, cumin, and pepper.
4. Stir in the cooked bacon.
5. Simmer on low for 1 hour, then serve.

Bev's Perfect Momelette

Season 1, Episode 6: ***Who Are You Going to Telephone?***

Breakfast is the most important meal of the day, and my special Momelette guarantees it's gonna be a good day. Like a bedazzled sweater, this recipe is really all about the accoutrements. They add the sizzle you need to really let your morning sparkle, whether you're power walking with the frentas, power washing the driveway, or power napping with your Murray. • *Yield: 2 servings*

2 tablespoons unsalted butter

1 large onion, diced

1 bell pepper, cored and diced

½ cup cubed ham

½ cup sliced mushrooms

4 eggs

¼ cup whole milk

Salt and pepper

½ cup grated cheddar cheese

1. In a skillet over medium-high heat, melt the butter and saute the onion and bell pepper until soft.
2. Add the ham and mushrooms to the skillet and cook for 5 minutes. Transfer the sauteed mixture to a dish and set aside. Do not clean the skillet.
3. In a bowl, whisk together the eggs and milk. Season with salt and pepper.
4. Pour the eggs into the same skillet over medium-low heat.
5. Spoon the sauteed mixture onto the eggs.
6. Cook for 1 minute, then add the cheese.
7. Fold the eggs over the fillings, then cover with a lid for 1 minute, or until the omelette is cooked through.

Ooey-Gooey Fudgy Chewies

SEASON 6, EPISODE 4: *Hersheypark*

When it comes to hobbies I've done it all: scrapbooking, jazzercise, water aerobics, bedazzling, water aerobics while bedazzling, watching my grown babies sleep at night, macramé, water macramé . . . but none of my hobbies are quite as delicious as baking. These chocolate bombs of love are the perfect way to welcome my snuggle monsters home after a long day at school. • *Yield: 24 cookies*

Butter for greasing

2½ cups powdered sugar

¾ cup cocoa powder

Pinch of salt

4 egg whites

1½ teaspoons vanilla extract

2 cups semisweet chocolate chips

1. Preheat the oven to 350°F. Line baking sheets with parchment paper and butter the parchment.
2. In a bowl, whisk together the powdered sugar, cocoa powder, and salt. Set aside.
3. In the bowl of a stand mixer with the whisk attachment, beat the egg whites until foamy.
4. With a spatula, fold the vanilla and the dry ingredients into the egg whites until just combined.
5. Fold in the chocolate chips.
6. Drop batter by tablespoonfuls onto the prepared pans.
7. Bake for 8 to 10 minutes, until the tops crackle. Let cool on the pan. Remove with a spatula.

Bev's Brownie Mood Boosters

Season 1, Episode 21: *The Age of Darkness*

When life gets tough, brownies get made—that's what I always say. Whether your babies are going through a breakup or struggling with a history paper, nothing puts a smile on their precious faces like a pan of my chocolatey-delicious brownies. Because if Mama can't fix it, she can fix them some sweetness. Also, it's 1980-something so therapy isn't a thing yet. • *Yield: 12 servings*

1 cup all-purpose flour, plus more for the pan

1 cup (2 sticks) unsalted butter, softened

2 cups sugar

4 eggs, lightly beaten

4 squares unsweetened Baker's chocolate, melted

½ teaspoon vanilla extract

1 cup chopped walnuts, optional

1. Preheat the oven to 350°F. Grease an 8 x 8-inch pan with nonstick spray and dust all sides with flour.
2. In a bowl, cream the butter and sugar.
3. Add the eggs and melted chocolate.
4. Stir in the flour until just combined.
5. Add the vanilla.
6. Fold in the walnuts, if using.
7. Pour into the prepared pan and bake for 30 to 35 minutes; do not overcook.
8. Let cool completely, then cut into squares to serve.

chapter 4

Entertaining the Bev Way

"Sorry, pickle, your end zone is now our brunch zone."

—BEVERLY GOLDBERG

Artichoke Dip

I'll admit: sometimes my kids get mad at me. And when that happens, the first thing I resort to is emotional blackmail, but when that doesn't work, I reach for my beloved artichoke dip recipe. They can't resist the dip and then they can't resist me. • *Yield: 10 servings*

3 (9-ounce) boxes frozen artichokes, thawed

1 cup mayonnaise

1 cup grated Parmesan cheese

1 teaspoon lemon juice

½ teaspoon white pepper

Crackers for serving

1. Preheat the oven to 350°F.
2. In a bowl, stir together the artichokes, mayonnaise, Parmesan cheese, lemon juice, and white pepper.
3. Pour the artichoke mixture into an 8 x 8-inch baking dish and bake for 20 minutes.
4. Serve with crackers.

"Rule #5: Mandatory hugs every time you walk through the door."

Bevy's Deceptively Healthy Mushroom Dip

The thing I love about my mushroom dip is how healthy it is. I mean the dip itself isn't healthy, but it's the perfect excuse to get your babies to eat their healthy veggies so they can grow big and strong and make you healthy babies of their own. It's a cycle.

• *Yield: 10 servings*

16 ounces white mushrooms

1 tablespoon Dijon mustard

1 tablespoon lemon juice

¾ teaspoon salt

⅛ teaspoon pepper

½ cup vegetable oil

4 green onions or scallions, chopped, plus more for decoration

Crackers, to serve

1. Preheat the oven to 400°F.
2. Place the mushrooms on a baking sheet and bake for 15 to 20 minutes, until soft.
3. Transfer the baked mushrooms to a blender or food processor and add the Dijon mustard, lemon juice, salt, and pepper. Blend until the dip just comes together, then continue to blend and drizzle in the oil. Transfer to a serving dish and stir in the green onions, then sprinkle more on top for decoration.
4. Refrigerate.
5. Serve cold with crackers.

Onion Dip

Season 1, Episode 20: *You're Not Invited*

You might remember this dip from when Adam served it at his make-out party. I know because I watched the whole thing from the closet where I was hiding. I think we can all agree, to be a great mom you gotta know how to make a great onion dip and how to spy on your children from a confined space. • *Yield: 10 servings*

2 (8-ounce) packages cream cheese, softened

1 cup sour cream

½ cup mayonnaise

2 (2-ounce) envelopes onion soup mix

½ cup grated Parmesan cheese

Crackers for serving

1. Preheat the oven to 400°F.
2. In a bowl, stir together the cream cheese, sour cream, mayonnaise, onion soup mix, and Parmesan cheese.
3. Spoon into an 8 x 8-inch baking dish and bake for 20 minutes.
4. Serve with crackers.

Mom-mosas

Season 5, Episode 17: *Colors*

There's no better way to celebrate Sunday Funday with your frentas than a couple of "Mom-mosas" in your fanciest brunch glassware. This sweet, bubbly beverage is the perfect way to really get the gossip flowing. • *Yield: 4 servings*

3 cups orange juice

1½ cups champagne

1 orange, sliced into rounds

1. Stir together the champagne and orange juice and pour into glasses.
2. Decorate with orange rounds.

Frozen Margs

It's not often that you get a night out with your husband, but when it does happen it's a cause for celebration! Mexican food and frozen margs are the best combo. Blend up a bunch and get ready for Taco Tuesday! • *Yield: 4 servings*

1 lime, halved

Kosher salt

3 cups ice

2 cups frozen strawberries

8 ounces tequila

1 cup frozen limeade concentrate

¼ cup triple sec

1. Rim glasses with the cut lime, then dip in salt. Set aside.
2. In a blender, combine the ice, frozen strawberries, tequila, limeade, and triple sec. Blend until slushy.
3. Pour into glasses to serve.

Bev's Chicken Salad

SEASON 2, EPISODE 16: *The Lost Boy*

I learned a lot from my mother about cooking, but her number one culinary commandment was that wasting food was not an option. So that forced me to get pretty creative about how I could turn leftovers into gotta-have-'ems. Now whenever I make chicken, I just toss any extras into my one-of-a-kind chicken salad, and believe me: it's so good, there are never any leftovers. • *Yield: 4 servings*

⅓ cup whole milk

3 tablespoons mayonnaise

2 tablespoons sweet relish

2 teaspoons honey mustard

2 cups diced, cooked chicken

½ cup dried cranberries

½ cup shredded carrots

1. In a large bowl, stir together the milk, mayonnaise, relish, and honey mustard.
2. Fold in the chicken, cranberries, and carrots.
3. Refrigerate until ready to serve.

"You just stay delicious, snuggle monster."

Ginzy Kremp's Cheese Triangles

Season 6, Episode 8: *The Living Room: A 100% True Story*

If your family is like mine, you know the living room is only for special occasions. It holds all my fanciest, velvety-est, dustiest furniture. So when I open it up for guests, I prepare my most sophisticated snacks and I always welcome them to bring elite treats of their own. That's how I first discovered Ginzy Kremp's Cheese Triangles. They were so delicious it practically ruined our friendship, but then her son and my daughter, Erica, started dating so I had to be civil. • *Yield: 10 servings*

2 cups shredded sharp cheddar cheese

½ pound bacon, cooked and chopped

1 small onion, quartered

2 tablespoons mayonnaise

1 teaspoon Worcestershire sauce

1 tablespoon ketchup

1 loaf thinly sliced white bread

1. Put the cheese, bacon, and onion in a food processor. Pulse until combined.
2. Add the mayonnaise and process until thickened into a spread. Transfer to a bowl.
3. Stir in the Worcestershire sauce and ketchup. Set aside.
4. Preheat the oven to 375°F.
5. Cut the crusts off the bread and cut the slices into triangles. Place on baking sheets.
6. Toast the triangles for 5 minutes until just crisp, not browned. Remove from the oven and let cool.
7. Decrease the oven temperature to 300°F.
8. Spread the cheese mixture onto the cooled toasts and bake for 12 to 15 minutes, until bubbly and slightly browned.
9. Let cool slightly, then serve.

Bev's Crab Cakes

Season 6, Episode 8: ***The Living Room: A 100% True Story***

Everything I make is a sign of my love for my family, but when I really want to make them feel the Bev-love I make seafood. Because as we all know, the fanciest, most expensive meat is the meat of the ocean, and when it comes to my family I spare no expense. • *Yield: 6 servings*

For the crab cakes:

Vegetable oil for greasing

1 pound crab meat

¼ cup seasoned breadcrumbs

⅔ cup mayonnaise

1 tablespoon honey mustard

1 teaspoon garlic powder

½ teaspoon celery salt

¼ teaspoon pepper

For the coating:

¾ cup seasoned breadcrumbs

¼ cup all-purpose flour

Make the crab cakes:

1. Preheat the oven to 350°F. Lightly grease a baking sheet with oil.
2. In a large bowl, mix together the crab meat, breadcrumbs, mayonnaise, honey mustard, garlic powder, celery salt, and pepper.
3. Form six hamburger-sized patties.

Make the coating:

1. In a shallow dish, mix together the breadcrumbs and flour.

Finish:

1. Roll the crab cake patties in the coating, and place on the prepared baking sheet.
2. Bake for 20 to 25 minutes, until golden brown.

Crusty Sausage Puffs

SEASON 5, EPISODE 17: ***Colors***

When I host a frenta brunch, I always pair my sweets with something savory like my crusty sausage puffs. These bite-size treats are the perfect appetizer for an afternoon of bedazzling, trading Tupperware, bedazzling that Tupperware, scrapbooking, bedazzling the scrapbooks, and gossiping about whose neighbor's sister's cousin-in-law's son got wait-listed at Brandeis. • *Yield: 24 puffs*

1 pound pork sausage, casings removed

½ cup diced onion

½ teaspoon garlic powder

½ teaspoon salt

¼ teaspoon onion powder

¼ teaspoon pepper

1 (17-ounce) package puff pastry sheets, thawed

1 egg, lightly beaten

¼ cup grated Parmesan cheese

1. Preheat the oven to 375°F. Grease two 12-cup muffin tins with nonstick spray.
2. In a skillet over medium-high heat, combine the sausage, onion, garlic powder, salt, onion powder, and pepper and cook until the sausage is browned. Set aside.
3. Lightly flour a work surface and unfold one sheet of puff pastry. Cut into 12 squares. Repeat with the second sheet for a total of 24.
4. Spoon a heaping tablespoon of the sausage mixture into the center of each square.
5. Brush the edges of the squares with the beaten egg, then fold the corners to the center to seal.
6. Place in the prepared muffin tin.
7. Brush the tops with more egg, then sprinkle with the Parmesan.
8. Bake for 20 minutes, until golden brown.
9. Let cool slightly, then serve.

Deviled Eggs for Your Angels

SEASON 3, EPISODE 21: *Rush*

My kids and I are so close, but every once in a while they want their "space." So that's when I whip up a batch of my devilishly good deviled eggs. My boofaloos just can't say no to them, so it's the perfect way to intrude on their lives and never leave, even if they ask politely. • *Yield: 6 servings*

8 eggs

3 to 4 tablespoons mayonnaise

1 tablespoon sweet relish

¼ teaspoon onion powder

¼ teaspoon paprika, plus more for sprinkling

¼ teaspoon salt

Pinch of pepper

Parsley for decoration

1. Place the eggs in a pot and cover them with 1 to 2 inches of water. Bring to a boil.
2. Turn off the heat, cover with a lid, and let sit for 12 minutes.
3. Transfer the eggs to an ice bath and let cool.
4. Once cooled, peel the eggs. Slice the peeled eggs in half lengthwise and scoop out the yolks.
5. In a bowl, stir together the egg yolks, mayonnaise, relish, onion powder, paprika, salt, and pepper.
6. Place the egg yolk mixture into a piping bag and pipe the filling into the egg white centers.
7. Sprinkle with more paprika and some parsley, to serve.

White Zin

White Zin is sometimes called a "mom wine," and what's wrong with that? If it's considered mom fuel, then fill up the ole Bev tank. Sure, it's affordable, fruity, and sweet—some people say it's barely wine—but anything that goes perfectly with Shrimp Parm is a beverage to be revered. A glass of White Zin every now and then is the perfect companion drink that goes well with all energetic activities.

What else would spark the creativity needed to bedazzle a sweater featuring a harlequin clown riding a unicorn while high-fiving a dolphin? Only White Zin, that's what.

And it's not just fashion that goes hand in hand with a glass of White Zin. Whether it's scrapbooking your schmoopaloos' baby pictures into glorious homages to their squishable, kissable youth, or planning the senior ski trip with your best frentas, it's a refreshing beverage that inspires your imagination, ingenuity, and resourcefulness. So raise a glass to mom wine and to smothers everywhere!

Naked Quiche

SEASON 6, EPISODE 8: ***The Living Room: A 100% True Story***

Does it even count as brunch if you don't have quiche? In my book, no. And in my cookbook, quiche is a big yes. It's the ultimate savory pie, and I've got the ultimate recipe. It's so good, I know I'll be friends with the frentas forever because, no matter how much I drive them up the wall, they'd never want to miss out on my quiche. • *Yield: 6 servings*

4 eggs

2 cups cottage cheese

1 cup shredded cheddar cheese

1 (10-ounce) package frozen broccoli, defrosted

Salt and pepper

1. Preheat the oven to 350°F. Grease a 9-inch pie pan with nonstick spray.
2. In a large bowl, beat the eggs, then stir in the cottage cheese, cheddar cheese, and broccoli. Season with salt and pepper.
3. Pour into the prepared pie dish and bake for 45 minutes, until cooked through and brown on top.

Cherry-Topped Ambrosia Salad

Season 1, Episode 9: ***Stop Arguing and Start Thanking***

These days when I hug my babies, they tend not to hug back because *apparently* they're not babies anymore. In fact, sometimes they recoil. That's when I make my signature Ambrosia Salad. They love it so much, they start serving up all the hugs my schmoo-loving heart desires. • *Yield: 8 servings*

12 ounces heavy cream

1½ cups sliced fresh strawberries

1 (11-ounce) can mandarin oranges, drained

1 (20-ounce) can crushed pineapple, drained

1 (15-ounce) can dark sweet cherries, drained

1. In the bowl of a stand mixer with the whisk attachment, whip the cream until soft peaks form. Set aside ½ cup.
2. Fold the strawberries, mandarin oranges, and pineapple into the remaining whipped cream.
3. Spoon into a serving dish and top with the reserved whipped cream. Top with the cherries.

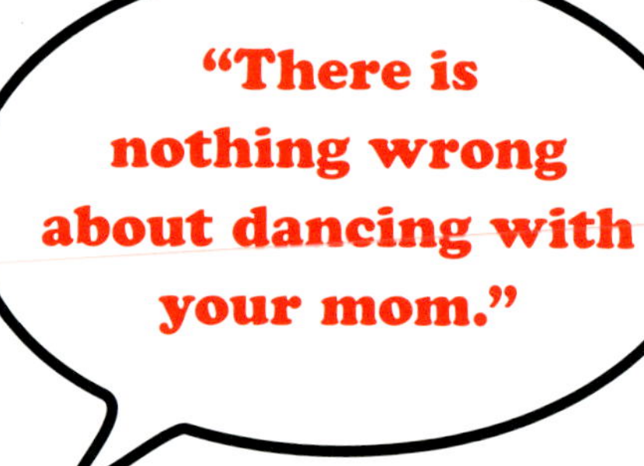

Fish Coquilles

When we host a dinner party (a rarity, since it would require Murray getting up from his chair), I know the easiest way to impress my guests is by serving seafood. And one of my favorite seafood delicacies is my fish coquilles. They come out so refined and delectable, they make my guests feel completely inferior—and that tastes pretty good to me. • *Yield: 10 servings*

You'll need:

10 baking sea shells

2 tablespoons vinegar

¼ teaspoon salt

1 pound cod fillets

4 tablespoons unsalted butter

½ cup sliced mushrooms

¼ cup diced green pepper

1 tablespoon minced onions

1¼ cups whole milk

¼ cup sherry

¼ cup all-purpose flour

½ teaspoon salt

¼ teaspoon garlic powder

¼ teaspoon dried marjoram

¼ teaspoon pepper

¾ cup breadcrumbs

¼ cup grated cheddar or Swiss cheese

Vegetable oil for greasing

1. In a skillet, bring ¾ cup water and the vinegar to a boil. Season the water with salt and add the fish fillets. Turn down the heat and cover, simmering until the fish is just cooked through, 7 to 8 minutes. Transfer the fish to a plate and discard the liquid.
2. Wipe out the pan. Over medium-high heat, melt 2 tablespoons of the butter. Saute the mushrooms, peppers, and onions until soft, about 5 minutes.
3. Add the milk, sherry, flour, salt, garlic powder, marjoram, and pepper. Bring to a boil and whisk until the mixture thickens, about 1 minute. Set aside.
4. Preheat the oven to 350°F.
5. Melt the remaining 2 tablespoons butter in a bowl in the microwave. Stir in the breadcrumbs and cheese.
6. Place the shells on a baking sheet. Lightly grease the shells with oil, and sprinkle 1 teaspoon of the breadcrumb mixture onto the bottom of each shell.

7. Flake the fish and spoon it evenly into the shells.

8. Top with the mushroom cream sauce.

9. Sprinkle the rest of the crumb mixture evenly on top of each of the filled shells.

10. Bake for 20 minutes, until browned.

“I am not flappy. I’m very flangry.”

—BEVERLY GOLDBERG

Veal Piccata

Season 6, Episode 17: ***Our Perfect Strangers***

This dish is a favorite of my Murray's. He absolutely loves veal. My daughter, Erica, on the other hand, is going through one of her "political" phases, so I do a chicken version for her. And when she decides to not be a pain in the you-know-where anymore, I'll get her back on the veal. Then she'll learn an important lesson they don't teach in college: trading in your moral high ground is worth it for a tasty veal. • *Yield: 4 servings*

4 veal cutlets

4 tablespoons (½ stick) unsalted butter

2 cloves garlic, cut in half

5 tablespoons all-purpose flour

Garlic powder

Salt and pepper

1 (8-ounce) can mushrooms

3 tablespoons white wine

4 thin lemon slices

1. Pound the veal out thin.
2. In a skillet over medium heat, melt the butter and add the garlic cloves.
3. In a shallow dish, whisk together the flour, garlic powder, salt, and pepper.
4. Dredge the cutlets in the flour mixture and cook until browned.
5. Remove the veal from the pan and discard the garlic.
6. Add the mushrooms and white wine to the pan, scraping the drippings.
7. Place the browned cutlets back in the pan and top each with a lemon slice.
8. Cover and cook for 8 to 10 minutes, until the veal is cooked through.

Carrot Cake

It's cake, it's vegetables, it's both! Carrot cake is a sweet and savory masterpiece, and I promise you mine is the best one you'll ever taste. You can thank me by telling your mother you love her and that she made you who you are today. This is a hint to my kids to call me. • *Yield: 12 servings*

For the cake:

2 cups all-purpose flour

2 teaspoons baking soda

2 teaspoons ground cinnamon

1 teaspoon salt

4 eggs

2 cups sugar

1½ cups vegetable oil

3 cups grated carrots

1 (8-ounce) can crushed pineapple with juice

½ cup chopped walnuts

½ cup golden raisins

½ cup flaked coconut

For the icing:

8 ounces powdered sugar

4 tablespoons (½ stick) unsalted butter, softened

3 ounces cream cheese, softened

1 teaspoon vanilla extract

Make the cake:

1. Preheat the oven to 350°F. Grease a tube pan with nonstick spray.
2. In a bowl, whisk together the flour, baking soda, cinnamon, and salt. Set aside.
3. In the bowl of a stand mixer with the beater attachment, beat the eggs, sugar, and oil.
4. Add the dry ingredients to the wet ingredients and beat until just combined.
5. Stir in the carrots and pineapple.
6. Pour half the batter into the prepared pan.
7. Into the remaining batter, stir the walnuts, raisins, and coconut. Pour on top of the other batter.
8. Bake for 50 minutes, until a toothpick inserted in the center comes out clean. Let cool completely in the pan before inverting the cake onto a plate.

Make the frosting:

1. In a bowl, stir together the powdered sugar, butter, cream cheese, and vanilla. Spread the icing over the cake to frost.
2. Refrigerate until ready to serve.

Raspberry Cheesecake

SEASON 5, EPISODE 11: ***The Goldberg Girls***

Not only is my Raspberry Cheesecake a dessert for the ages, it's also a trap. Yup, it's a delicious and sneaky way of getting my Murray to eat fresh fruit. Murray can't stand fruit. He says it's "drippy" and "slippery" and "what's with all the seeds?" But just wrap that fruit in some cheesecake and he's on board. He falls for this trick every time and it makes this cheesecake even sweeter. • *Yield: 12 servings*

For the crust:

2 cups graham cracker crumbs

6 tablespoons unsalted butter, melted

¼ cup sugar

For the filling:

3 (8-ounce) packages cream cheese, softened

3 eggs

1 cup sugar

1 teaspoon vanilla extract

For the topping:

1 cup sour cream

2 tablespoons sugar

1 teaspoon vanilla extract

12 ounces raspberries

Make the crust:

1. Preheat the oven to 350°F. Grease a 9-inch springform pan with nonstick spray.
2. In a bowl combine the graham cracker crumbs, melted butter, and sugar.
3. Press into the bottom and partially up the sides of the prepared pan. Bake the crust for 10 minutes. Remove from the oven but leave the oven on.
4. Let cool, then wrap the bottom and sides of the pan with a large piece of aluminum foil. Set aside.

Make the filling:

1. Ready a water bath by boiling a pot of water.
2. In the bowl of a stand mixer with the beater attachment, beat the cream cheese, eggs, sugar, and vanilla until just combined. Pour into the prebaked crust.

3. Place the foil-wrapped pan inside of a large roasting pan and place in the oven. Pour the hot water into the roasting pan approximately 1-inch up the side of the pan, being careful not to spill into the cheesecake.
4. Bake for 55 to 60 minutes.
5. Remove from the oven and let stand for 15 minutes.

Make the topping:

1. In a bowl, stir together the sour cream, sugar, and vanilla. Spread the sour cream mixture over the cheesecake and bake for an additional 10 minutes.
2. Let cool completely, then refrigerate overnight.
3. Run a knife around the edges of the springform pan before releasing.
4. Place on a serving plate and decorate with the fresh raspberries around the base to serve.

Snickerdoodles

Season 4, Episode 19: ***A Night to Remember***

A lot of wives feel like they can't get their husbands to do what they want. But not me. I know that if you just snicker a doodle, you can get your husband to do just about anything: take you out to dinner, mow the lawn, tell you he loves you. And if the snickers are extra-doodled, you might even get him to put on pants. • *Yield: 20 cookies*

2¾ cups all-purpose flour

2 teaspoons cream of tartar

1 teaspoon baking soda

Pinch of salt

1 cup (2 sticks) unsalted butter, softened

1¾ cups sugar

2 eggs

1 teaspoon vanilla extract

2 tablespoons ground cinnamon

1. Preheat the oven to 400°F. Line baking sheets with parchment paper.
2. In a large bowl whisk together the flour, cream of tartar, baking soda, and salt.
3. In the bowl of a stand mixer with the paddle attachment, cream the butter and 1½ cups of the sugar.
4. Beat in the eggs and vanilla.
5. Add the dry ingredients to the wet ingredients and beat until the dough just comes together.
6. In a small bowl mix together the remaining ¼ cup sugar and the cinnamon.
7. Roll the dough into 1-inch balls, then each ball roll in the cinnamon-sugar mixture. Place on the prepared baking sheets, 2 inches apart.
8. Bake for 8 minutes. Let cool slightly, then transfer to a wire rack to cool completely.

chapter 5

Goldberg Holiday Traditions

"I give you my everything three hundred and sixty-four days of the year. Is it too much to ask to have one day where you do something for me?"

—BEVERLY GOLDBERG

Essie Karp's Brussels Sprouts

Season 6, Episode 13: ***I Coulda Been a Lawyer***

Around the holidays, I love trading recipes with my frentas, Linda Schwartz, Gina Kremp, and, of course, Essie Karp. Essie is a fantastic cook, I mean not as good as me, that would be impossible. But if I'm gonna let one of her recipes into my book it's going to be her Brussels sprouts. I don't have a Brussels sprouts recipe of my own because veggies are not my family's thing, though if I did have one it would be better than Essie's. But I let her have this.

• *Yield: 10 servings*

¼ cup pecan halves

2 (12-ounce) bags frozen Brussels sprouts, thawed

2 tablespoons olive oil

½ cup dried cranberries

1½ tablespoons maple syrup

1 tablespoon balsamic vinegar

¼ teaspoon vanilla extract

Salt and pepper

1. In a dry skillet over medium heat, toast the pecans until lightly golden. Set aside.
2. Preheat the oven to 400°F.
3. On a baking sheet, toss the Brussels sprouts in the olive oil.
4. Bake for 15 to 20 minutes.
5. In a large bowl, toss the roasted Brussels sprouts with the cranberries and toasted pecans.
6. In a small bowl, whisk together the maple syrup, balsamic vinegar, and vanilla.
7. Pour the dressing over the sprouts mixture, tossing to coat.
8. Season with salt and pepper.

Linda Schwartz's Cranberry Gelatin Mold

Season 2, Episode 8: ***I Rode a Hoverboard***
Season 4, Episode 23: ***Jedi Master Adam Skywalker***

Yes, it's a Beverly Goldberg cookbook, but who's Beverly Goldberg without her frentas? This is Linda Schwartz's recipe from her mother-in-law Sylvia, who passed away many years ago. (So sad. I sent a huge floral arrangement.) Gelatin molds are very in right now, and they're good for the holidays, birthdays, or your classic mid-morning gelatin snack. • *Yield: 8 servings*

You'll need:

1 (6½-cup) gelatin mold

2 (3-ounce) packages cherry gelatin

¾ cup sugar

2 cups hot water, plus 1 cup cold water

2 tablespoons lemon juice

Pinch of salt

1½ cups coarsely ground cranberries

1 (8-ounce) can pineapple tidbits, drained

1 cup mandarin oranges, drained

¾ cup chopped celery

⅓ cup chopped walnuts

1. In a bowl stir together the cherry gelatin powder and sugar with the hot water. Mix until the gelatin is dissolved.
2. Stir in the cold water, lemon juice, and salt.
3. Place the gelatin mixture in the refrigerator until soft set, about 1 hour.
4. Stir in the cranberries, pineapple, mandarin oranges, celery, and walnuts.
5. Spray the mold with nonstick spray, then pour in the mixture.
6. Refrigerate the gelatin for 4 hours, or until firm.
7. Dip the mold three-fourths of the way into warm water for a few seconds to loosen. Unmold to serve.

Matzo Brei

Season 6, Episode 11: ***The Wedding Singer***

If I ever see Murray pick up a spatula or mixing bowl in the kitchen, I know we're in trouble. When it comes to reading recipes, he might as well be illiterate. He can't tell flour from baking soda, olive oil from vegetable oil, or sugar from salt. But there is one thing he knows how to make: his matzo brei. I don't know how he does it. Just kidding, yes I do. It's all in this recipe below.

• *Yield: 4 servings*

1 box regular matzo

4 tablespoons (½ stick) unsalted butter

5 eggs, lightly beaten

1. Wet the matzo sheets with water. Set aside and let soften.
2. Melt the butter in a skillet over medium heat.
3. Break the matzo into pieces and add to the pan. Saute until browned.
4. Add the eggs and scramble the mixture until the eggs are just set.
5. Serve immediately.

Latkes

SEASON 6, EPISODE 10: ***Yippee Ki Yay Melon Farmer***

When it comes to Hanukkah, latkes are the star of the show. As my Barry puts it, they're delicious golden-brown hockey pucks, and if you don't get the latkes right your Hanukkah is nothing. But with this recipe your schmoos will be begging for eight days and eight nights of fried potato-y goodness. Oh, and watch out for oil burns. Nothing ruins Hanukkah faster than a trip to the doctor. Though if you do go, pack extra latkes. He'll probably charge you less. • *Yield: 4 servings*

2 large russet potatoes

1 onion

1 egg

⅓ cup matzo meal

1 teaspoon baking powder

1 teaspoon salt

1 teaspoon sugar

Vegetable oil for frying

Applesauce for serving

1. Grate the potatoes and put them in a large bowl.
2. Grate the onion and add to the potatoes.
3. Stir in the egg, matzo meal, baking powder, salt, and sugar.
4. Form the potato mixture into patties.
5. In a skillet over medium-high heat, heat 2 inches of oil and fry the patties until golden brown.
6. Serve with applesauce.

Barry's Orange Potatoes with Marshmallows

SEASON 2, EPISODE 7: *A Goldberg Thanksgiving*

As you know by now, Barry's not a big fan of veggies. So when I showed him that you can throw a giant layer of ooey-gooey marshmallow on top of sweet potatoes and it still technically counts as a veggie, he became president of the sweet potato fan club. • *Yield: 10 servings*

3 (15-ounce) cans sweet potatoes, drained

1 cup sugar

⅓ cup bourbon

½ cup (1 stick) unsalted butter, melted

½ teaspoon vanilla extract

2 cups mini marshmallows

1. Preheat the oven to 350°F. Prepare a 9 x 13-inch baking dish with nonstick spray.
2. In a bowl, mash the sweet potatoes with the sugar, bourbon, butter, and vanilla.
3. Pour into the baking dish and top with the marshmallows.
4. Bake for 30 minutes, until the marshmallows are browned.

FRESH
FARM FRESH
Milk
Grade A
QUART (946 ml)

Mashed Potatoes

SEASON 3, EPISODE 3: ***Jimmy 5 Is Alive***

Thanksgiving is supposed to be about family's coming together, but when it comes to my family, the only way to get them all in one room is with the perfect mashed potatoes. I make mine so thick and creamy you could use it as stucco. It's the potato glue that keeps my family all under one roof during the holidays. • *Yield: 8 servings*

6 russet potatoes, peeled and quartered

1 (16-ounce) container sour cream

1 (0.9-ounce) package green onion dip mix

1 (8-ounce) package cream cheese, softened

½ cup (1 stick) unsalted butter, softened

⅓ cup heavy cream

1 teaspoon garlic salt

1 teaspoon paprika

1. Bring a large pot of water to a boil. Carefully add the potatoes and cook for 15 minutes, or until tender. Drain.
2. Preheat the oven to 350°F. Grease a large baking dish with nonstick spray.
3. In the bowl of a stand mixer with the beater attachment, stir together the cooked potatoes, sour cream, green onion dip mix, cream cheese, butter, heavy cream, and garlic salt until smooth.
4. Spoon into the prepared dish and sprinkle with paprika.
5. Bake for 30 minutes.

Bill Lewis's Fried-Stuffing Balls

Season 4, Episode 7: ***Ho-ly K.I.T.T.***

My Murray isn't the most social guy, but he does have one best friend named Bill Lewis. There are three things you need to know about Bill: he collects cars, he's a big softy who cries easily, and he's a nice guy who knows how to make a mean fried-stuffing ball.

• *Yield: 10 servings*

3 cups cooked stuffing

⅔ cup all-purpose flour

1 teaspoon garlic powder

¼ teaspoon onion powder

2 eggs

1 cup seasoned breadcrumbs

Vegetable oil for frying

Salt and pepper

1. Use a scoop to form the stuffing into 2½-inch-round balls. Set aside.
2. In a shallow dish, whisk together the flour, garlic powder, and onion powder.
3. Lightly beat the eggs in another shallow dish. Put the breadcrumbs in a third dish.
4. Dredge the stuffing balls in the seasoned flour, then the eggs, then finally the breadcrumbs.
5. In a skillet over medium-high heat, heat 2 inches of oil and fry the balls until golden brown. Transfer them to a plate lined with paper towels to drain and season with salt and pepper.

Noodle Kugel

Season 5, Episode 16: ***The Scrunchie Rule***

Some people think the holidays are about love and togetherness, but I know they're really about competition and winning. So as the kids get older and don't want to come home for the holidays, I use my noodle kugel as my winning recipe to get them all under my roof. And now, every year, my house is the holiday house. • *Yield: 8 servings*

1 (16-ounce) package medium egg noodles

1 (16-ounce) container small curd cottage cheese with pineapple

1 (8-ounce) container sour cream

4 tablespoons (½ stick) unsalted butter, melted, plus 2 tablespoons softened

⅔ cup plus ½ cup sugar

1 tablespoon plus 2 teaspoons cinnamon

3 teaspoons vanilla extract

4 eggs

2 cups corn flakes, crushed

1. Preheat the oven to 350°F. Grease a 2-quart baking dish with nonstick spray.
2. Cook the noodles until al dente, according to package directions. Drain and transfer to a large bowl.
3. To the cooked noodles, add the cottage cheese, sour cream, melted butter, ⅔ cup of the sugar, 1 tablespoon of the cinnamon, and the vanilla. Stir.
4. Add the eggs and stir to combine.
5. Pour the noodle mixture into the prepared dish.
6. In a separate bowl, stir together the crushed corn flakes and the remaining ½ cup sugar and 2 teaspoons cinnamon.
7. Spread the cornflake mixture on top of the noodle mixture.
8. Cut up the 2 tablespoons softened butter and evenly distribute the pieces around the top of the casserole.
9. Bake for 1 hour and 15 minutes, until golden brown.

Nana's Stuffing

Season 2, Episode 7: ***A Goldberg Thanksgiving***

It's simply not a Thanksgiving meal without a tummy-stuffing mountain of stuffing. And what makes my recipe extra special is that it's been passed down through generations. I got it from my mama, Irene Solomon, and my babies will make it for their babies, and if they don't want to, well then, I'll just have to come over and make it for them and maybe stay over for a few days... or weeks. Ya know, stuffing takes time. • *Yield: 8 servings*

2½ cups seasoned bread cubes

6 eggs, lightly beaten

2 tablespoons garlic powder

Salt and pepper

1. In a large bowl, stir together the seasoned bread cubes, eggs, and garlic powder.
2. Season well with salt and pepper.
3. Right before roasting, spoon the stuffing mixture into the turkey cavity.
4. Close the opening and roast the turkey as usual (see page 128), cooking the stuffing until an instant-read thermometer reaches 165°F.

"Come on, lazy buns, let's earn that stuffing!"

Thanksgiving Turkey

SEASON 2, EPISODE 7: ***A Goldberg Thanksgiving***

Over the years I've made Thanksgiving turkey a variety of ways—ballotine, roulade, spatchcocked. Bill Lewis even tried to deep-fry one once and we know how that worked out. Sometimes a good old traditional roast turkey is all you need. • *Yield: 8 to 10 servings*

1 (12- to 15-pound) turkey

½ cup (1 stick) unsalted butter, softened

1 tablespoon minced garlic

1 tablespoon salt

2 teaspoons pepper

1 onion, quartered

Nana's Stuffing (page 127), optional

1. Preheat the oven to 350°F.
2. Remove the neck and giblets from inside the turkey cavity.
3. Rinse the turkey and pat dry, then place in a roasting pan.
4. In a small bowl, mash the butter with the garlic and rub it onto the turkey, over and under the skin, and inside. Season with the salt and pepper.
5. Place the quartered onion inside the turkey, add the stuffing, if using, then truss the legs.
6. Tent a piece of aluminum foil over the turkey. Bake for 2½ to 3 hours.
7. Uncover, then cook for another hour until the thickest part of the thigh reachcs 180°F and the internal temperature of the stuffing reaches 165°F.
8. Let the turkey sit for 15 minutes, then transfer the stuffing to a bowl, if using, and carve the turkey.

Rugelach

Season 3, Episode 3: ***Jimmy 5 Is Alive***

Rugelach is a sweet pastry, so whenever my friends are getting salty, I pull out my rugelach recipe. It's the perfect thing to keep their frenta-mouths full, so I'm the one who gets to do all the talking. And I wouldn't have it any other way. • *Yield: 4 dozen cookies*

For the dough:

2 cups (4 sticks) unsalted butter, softened

1 (8-ounce) package cream cheese, softened

4 cups all-purpose flour

4 tablespoons sugar

3 tablespoons sour cream

1 teaspoon salt

For the filling and to finish:

¼ cup sugar

1 teaspoon ground cinnamon

2 cups filling (raisins, chopped nuts, mixed jelly, or mini chocolate chips)

2 egg whites plus 1 tablespoon sugar for glaze

Make the dough:

1. In a bowl, mix together the butter, cream cheese, flour, sugar, sour cream, and salt until the dough just comes together. Divide into four discs, wrap in plastic wrap, and refrigerate overnight.
2. Preheat the oven to 375°F. Line baking sheets with parchment paper.
3. On a floured surface, roll out one dough round to a ¼-inch thickness.

Make the filling:

1. In a small bowl, stir together the sugar and cinnamon. Sprinkle one-fourth of the mixture evenly onto the rolled-out dough.

To finish:

1. Spread the filling of your choice over the dough. Cut into 12 wedges.
2. Starting at the long end, roll to form a crescent. Place on the prepared baking sheets.
3. Repeat with the other three dough discs.
4. In a small bowl, whisk together the egg whites and sugar, then brush on the rugelach.
5. Bake for 25 to 30 minutes, until golden brown. Let cool on a wire rack.

Mandel Bread

It goes without saying that in my house food is love. That's why, when I need an extra helping of Adam's love, I make mandel bread. He can't resist this twice-baked delicious treat, and I can't resist the twice-squeezed hugs he gives me after a fresh batch.

• *Yield: 48 cookies*

3 heaping cups all-purpose flour

1 tablespoon baking powder

¼ teaspoon salt

3 eggs

1⅓ cups sugar

¾ cup vegetable oil

1 teaspoon vanilla extract

1 cup semisweet chocolate chips (nuts or raisins can also be substituted)

2 egg yolks plus 2 tablespoons water for egg wash

Ground cinnamon for dusting

1. In a bowl, whisk together the flour, baking powder, and salt. Set aside.
2. In a separate bowl, mix together the eggs, sugar, oil, and vanilla.
3. Add the dry ingredients to the wet ingredients and mix until the dough just comes together, then stir in the chocolate chips.
4. Shape the dough into two logs and wrap in plastic wrap. Refrigerate for 2 to 4 hours.
5. Preheat the oven to 350°F. Place the dough logs on baking sheets lined with parchment paper.
6. Brush the logs with the egg wash and sprinkle with cinnamon.
7. Bake for 20 to 25 minutes.
8. Cool slightly, then slice each log into 24 pieces.
9. Place the cut pieces back on the baking sheets and bake for another 10 minutes, until dry and crisp.

"My job is done. Maybe it's time for you to do your jobs and spend the next few hours thinking about the thing or person that you're most thankful for."

—BEVERLY GOLDBERG

Apple Crisp

Season 2, Episode 7: ***A Goldberg Thanksgiving***

When I look at my kids, all I can think is I just want to eat you up. I literally want to consume your squishy tushies. But since that's not allowed, the next best thing is to eat up a piping hot serving of my apple crisp. It's almost as sweet as Adam's delicious neck meat, and the cleanup is much faster! • *Yield: 6 servings*

---

4 apples, peeled, cored, and thinly sliced

2 teaspoons ground cinnamon

6 tablespoons unsalted butter, softened and cut into cubes

½ cup all-purpose flour, sifted

½ cup sugar

Whipped cream, for serving

1. Preheat the oven to 375°F. Grease an 8 x 8-inch baking dish with nonstick spray.
2. In a bowl, toss the apples, ½ cup water, and the cinnamon. Pour into the prepared baking dish.
3. In a separate bowl, mix together the butter, flour, and sugar until the pieces are no larger than a pea.
4. Crumble the mixture over the apples.
5. Bake for 45 minutes, until golden brown.
6. Serve the crisp with whipped cream.

Hamantaschen

Season 5, Episode 19: ***Flashy Little Flashdancer***

If you think Murray's not a cook, well his father, Ben, is even worse. But he has given us one recipe: his delightful hamantaschens. He brings them over every year, and then immediately eats them all. But they're so good, who can blame him? • *Yield: 18 to 24 cookies*

2½ cups all-purpose flour, plus more for dusting

½ cup sugar

1½ teaspoons baking powder

Pinch of salt

2 eggs

⅓ cup orange juice

¼ cup vegetable oil

1 teaspoon vanilla extract

1 cup fruit preserves (prunes, cherries, blueberries, apples)

1. In a bowl, whisk together the flour, sugar, baking powder, and salt.
2. Make a well in the center of the dry ingredients and stir in the eggs, orange juice, oil, and vanilla.
3. When the dough comes together, wrap it in plastic wrap and refrigerate for 10 to 15 minutes.
4. Preheat the oven to 350°F. Line a baking sheet with parchment paper.
5. On a floured surface, roll out the dough ¼ inch thick, then use a round cookie cutter or a glass to cut out 4-inch circles.
6. Place ½ teaspoon of fruit preserves into the center of each circle.
7. Fold three sides over into the shape of a triangle and pinch closed.
8. Bake for 12 to 15 minutes, until golden brown. Let cool on a wire rack.

chapter 6

Recipes from the Old Country

"The Bevernator stops for no one."

—BEVERLY GOLDBERG

Old Country Sweet-and-Sour Balls

My mother, Irene, came from the old country, where you cooked everything from scratch. I treasured her recipes, but I'm a modern 1980-something woman so I know good ole canned and packaged food is just as delicious and a heck of a lot quicker. So this dish is a new country spin on an old country favorite. • *Yield: 6 servings*

1½ pounds ground beef

1 pound ground pork

1 egg

½ cup matzo meal

¼ cup cold water

½ cup ketchup

1 teaspoon garlic powder

½ teaspoon salt

¼ teaspoon pepper

1 (10.75-ounce) can tomato soup

1 (14-ounce) can cranberry sauce

2 tablespoons brown sugar

2 tablespoons lemon juice

1. In a bowl, mix together the ground beef, ground pork, egg, matzo meal, cold water, ketchup, garlic powder, salt, and pepper.
2. Form into 2½-inch meatballs. Set aside.
3. In a Dutch oven, stir together the tomato soup, cranberry sauce, brown sugar, and lemon juice.
4. Bring the sauce to a simmer, then add the meatballs.
5. Cover and simmer on low for 1½ hours.

Pop's Red Beet Borscht

Season 2, Episode 2: *Mama Drama*

My father Al "Pops" Solomon was a sweet man who happened to love this sour soup. My dad would jump at any opportunity for borscht: borscht for dinner, borscht at lunch, breakfast borscht? For Albert Solomon, why not? And Murray loves it too. It's typically served with sour cream, but Murray puts crumbled matzo on it. And here's a trade secret: use canned beets—no one will know the difference, and you can use the money you save on a tasteful fashion-apron with shoulder pads! • *Yield: 8 servings*

3 to 4 pounds bone-in beef short ribs

6 to 9 red whole beets, grated

4 onions, diced

1 cup sugar

1 tablespoon lemon juice

3 or 4 cloves garlic, smashed

1 large head cabbage, sliced

1. Place 4 quarts water and the short ribs in a large Dutch oven and bring to a boil. Remove the schmutz that rises to the top. Lower the heat to medium-high, then cover and simmer for 10 minutes.
2. Add the beets and onions and simmer for another 10 minutes.
3. Stir in the sugar, lemon juice, garlic, and cabbage.
4. Cook the borscht for 15 minutes until the cabbage is tender.

Grandma's Unbeatable Blintzes

As a girl, I learned how to make blintzes from the best: my grandmother. I watched her slave for hours just to blintz the perfect blintz. And I can't wait to pass this recipe on to my children. And then have them not make them because they never listen to me and, apparently, I failed as a mother. I guess I'll just make them myself and mail them the blintzes like my grandmother intended. • *Yield: 6 servings*

1 cup all-purpose flour

½ teaspoon salt

4 eggs, beaten, plus 1 yolk

1 cup whole milk

Unsalted butter for the pan, plus 1 tablespoon melted

16 ounces cottage cheese, drained

1 tablespoon sugar

Pinch of salt

1. In a bowl whisk together the flour and salt and make a well in the center.
2. Add the whole eggs and milk, stirring constantly until smooth.
3. Pass the batter through a strainer to get rid of the lumps. Let rest for 10 minutes.
4. Grease a 6-inch nonstick skillet over medium-high heat with butter and add just enough batter to thinly coat the bottom of the pan. Cook the crepe until browned lightly on the bottom. Transfer to a plate and repeat with the rest of the batter.
5. In a bowl, stir together the cottage cheese, the egg yolk, melted butter, sugar, and salt.
6. Place 3 tablespoons of filling in the center of the browned side of the crepe. Raise the bottom flap to cover the filling, then pull the top flap over the bottom and tuck the sides under until almost touching.
7. Add more butter to the same skillet and place the blintz in the pan, flipping when lightly browned.
8. Repeat steps 6 and 7 with the rest of the crepes.

GAMES

Paprikás Krumpli

Ah, stew or, as I think of it, soup that makes you work. This recipe was brought over by a relative from the old country named Gleb. How exactly are we related? It's not clear, but what is crystal clear is this stew is spicy, flavorful, and delicious. • *Yield: 6 servings*

1 onion, diced

2 tablespoons olive oil

4 potatoes, cut into small cubes

1 tomato, diced

½ cup diced green pepper

1 clove garlic, minced

1 teaspoon paprika

1 teaspoon ground caraway seeds

1 teaspoon salt

½ teaspoon pepper

1. In a Dutch oven over medium-high heat, saute the onion in the olive oil until softened.
2. Stir in the potatoes, tomato, green pepper, garlic, paprika, caraway seeds, salt, and pepper. Add enough water to just cover the vegetables.
3. Bring to a boil. Simmer until the potatoes are tender, 10 to 15 minutes.

"I need to command respect with my giant hair."

Bev's Perfect (Cold Cut) Slice

You don't wake up at 5 a.m. to give your kids lunch money, no sir. You wake up at the crack of dawn to gather up all the ingredients necessary for creating a symphony of sandwiches to nourish your children's empty tummies.

- **When it comes to making your schmoopies' school lunch,** it's all about making sure your cold cuts are the perfect thickness, and the only way to get those sandwiches just right is to head straight to the deli counter and ask for the commercial-grade industrial slicer. Too low on the slicer dial and you'll be saddled with paper-thin slices that are barely usable. Too high on the dial will give you slices as thick as your thumb, which is just a choking hazard waiting to happen. The little fruits of your loins' windpipes are only so big and your slices should be easily digestible.

  This means asking the deli counter for a nice medium-low on the dial. This will give you the perfect thickness to taste all the savory, meaty goodness, whether you're piling up a mile-high pastrami on rye, or building a skyscraper of salami on sourdough.

- **A word of warning:** Slicer thicknesses vary by store, so unless you go to the same deli counter every time, don't you dare take them at their word; be sure to always ask for a sample, and bring a ruler. That way you'll know the exact width of your favorite meats down to the millimeter.

Stuffed Cabbage

Season 3, Episode 10: ***A Christmas Story***

Stuffed cabbage is a basic recipe made by many Jewish and Polish cooks, and everyone has her own way of making it. My Polish friend's secret was to add strips of bacon right before baking; it added so much flavor that I've been making it her way ever since. While you're supposed to throw out the bacon before serving, Murray always insists on eating it. He is often like my human garbage can. And if he doesn't want it, our dog, Lucky, does. • *Yield: 6 servings*

1 head green cabbage

1 pound ground beef

1 pound ground veal

1 pound ground pork

1 tablespoon garlic powder

1 teaspoon salt

1 teaspoon pepper

8 to 10 strips of bacon (1 strip per cabbage roll)

3 (15-ounce) cans crushed tomatoes

1 cup brown sugar

½ cup lemon juice

1. In a pot of boiling water, cook the entire head of cabbage for 2 to 4 minutes, until softened, separating the leaves as they cook (use tongs). Drain.
2. Preheat the oven to 350°F. Grease a 9 x 13-inch pan with nonstick spray.
3. In a bowl, mix together the beef, veal, pork, garlic powder, salt, and pepper.
4. Lay out the leaves and add a scoop of the meat mixture to each. Tuck in the sides of the cabbage leaves and roll them up. Place the rolls in the prepared pan, seam side down.
5. Place a strip of bacon on top of each roll.
6. In a bowl stir together the tomatoes, brown sugar, and lemon juice.
7. Pour the sauce on top and bake for 45 minutes, until cooked through.

The Delish Knish

SEASON 5, EPISODE 18: ***MTV Spring Break***

The Goldberg family has a complicated relationship with knishes. I've made several delicious knishes in my day—so delicious, in fact, that my two oldest, Barry and Erica, had the bright idea to steal some knishes from my father's pool grill down in Florida. And they got arrested for it. But I guess if you'd grown up eating my knishes, you'd steal for them too. • *Yield: 12 servings*

For the dough:

1¾ cups all-purpose flour, plus more for dusting

1½ tablespoons vegetable oil

1 tablespoon sugar

½ teaspoon baking powder

1 egg

Pinch of salt

For the filling:

1 (16-ounce container) cottage cheese

2 egg yolks

2 teaspoons sugar

1 tablespoon cream cheese

1 teaspoon grated lemon zest

Make the dough:

1. Preheat the oven to 350°F. Line baking sheets with parchment paper.
2. In a bowl, stir together the flour, ½ cup water, the oil, sugar, baking powder, egg, and salt. Mix until just combined.
3. Sprinkle flour over a clean surface. Roll the dough out to a ¼-inch thickness and cut into 3-inch rounds.

Make the filling:

1. In a medium bowl, stir together the cottage cheese, egg yolks, sugar, cream cheese, and lemon zest.

Assemble and bake:

1. To each piece of dough, add a spoonful of filling, then fold the edges up, and pinch closed.
2. Place on the prepared baking sheets and bake for 40 to 45 minutes, until golden brown.

Marlene's Moist Apple Cake

Between me and my sister, Marlene, I was the cook in the family. I mean, between me and anyone's sister, I'm the cook. But Marlene has one recipe for apple cake that is so yummy, I make it all the time. Just don't tell her that. • *Yield: 10 servings*

4 apples, peeled, cored, and sliced

1 cup golden raisins

2 teaspoons ground cinnamon mixed with 4 teaspoons sugar

2¾ cups all-purpose flour

1 tablespoon baking powder

½ teaspoon salt

1¾ cups sugar

1 cup vegetable oil

⅔ cup orange juice

4 eggs

2 teaspoons vanilla extract

1. In a medium bowl, toss together the apples, raisins, and the cinnamon-sugar mixture. Set aside.
2. Preheat the oven to 350°F. Grease a Bundt pan with nonstick spray.
3. In another medium bowl, whisk together the flour, baking powder, and salt. Set aside.
4. In a large bowl, stir together the sugar, oil, orange juice, eggs, and vanilla.
5. Add the dry ingredients to the wet ingredients and stir until just combined.
6. Pour 1 cup of batter into the pan and top with one-third of the apple mixture.
7. Add half of the remaining batter on top.
8. Then layer on the rest of the apple mixture.
9. Evenly spread the rest of the batter on top and place the Bundt pan on a baking sheet.
10. Bake for 60 to 75 minutes, or until cooked through and a skewer comes out clean.

Epilogue

by Adam F. Goldberg

When I sat down to write *The Goldbergs*, my goal was to make a comedic exposé of surviving a crazy family with no boundaries. I thought I was the only kid on the planet who had a grouchy dad that dropped his pants at the door and a snuggle-starved mother who stormed down to school to yell at my teachers every week. But then . . . something unexpected happened—the audience saw their family in mine. Turns out, I wasn't writing an exposé. I was just writing about the common experience of surviving the eighties.

The series began exploring my sixth-grade year, and it was a rough one. I had a crooked bowl cut, screechy voice, and giant Steve Urkel glasses to correct my lazy eye. It was the year I got the nickname "Goldnerd" on the school bus. Granted, it was well deserved. But it still hurt.

Never in my wildest dreams did I ever imagine that there would one day be a TV show about my most cringeworthy moments. But even better, our most dedicated fans nicknamed themselves The Goldnerds. That's right, my childhood nickname that made my heart sink is now my greatest source of pride. In fact, this book wouldn't even exist if it wasn't for all the Goldnerds out there. Literally. For the last six years, you've constantly tweeted my mom, asking to have her heart-clogging, cheese-covered recipes. You got her so riled up that I had no choice but to help her release this book. So thank you, Goldnerds. You did it!

Writing about my family, friends, and teachers for the last seven years has been an exhausting and stressful blur—but it's also been exhilarating and rewarding beyond words. None of it would be possible without my insanely talented cast. I'm truly blessed to have Wendi, Jeff, George, Troy, Hayley, Sean, AJ, and Sam working tirelessly every week to bring my scripts to life. I'd also like to thank ABC for their continued support, especially Jodie and Vicki for all of their help in the trenches. I'd like to thank my brilliant producer, Doug Robinson, who insisted the world would watch *The Goldbergs* when I insisted they wouldn't. It's crazy to think that we've now made more than 150 episodes—only made possible due to my wonderful line producer Annette Davis and my hilarious writing staff, now led by Bishy and Barnow. I'd also like to thank my beautiful wife for having the biggest heart on the planet. But most of all, I'd like to thank my family. The hardest thing about making this show is that my dad isn't here to see it. If he was still here, I know he'd call me up and say, "Who knew? You're not a total moron!" That's Murray Goldberg's way of saying "You did good, kiddo." Miss you every day, Mur-Man.

JTP!

—Adam F. Goldberg

Twitter @adamfgoldberg

Index

(Page references in italics refer to illustrations.)

About the Authors

Beverly Goldberg is the real-life mom of *The Goldbergs* creator and showrunner, Adam F. Goldberg. She has been compiling her recipe collection for decades. She is excited to finally get to share all of her culinary secrets and amusing family anecdotes in this cookbook.

Jenn Fujikawa, co-author and food photographer, is a lifestyle and pop culture writer for StarWars.com, Marvel.com, Nerdist, Amy Poehler's Smart Girls, and more. Unique family dinners and geeky baking are a staple of her website www.justjennrecipes.com, and her recipes have been featured on *Buzzfeed*, the *LA Times*, *Sanrio*, *Woman's Day*, and the cover of *Food Network Magazine*.